Jumbo
Coloring Pad
Tiere

Coloring Pages for Kids

Coloring Pages for Kids
An imprint of Ciparum LLC

Jumbo Coloring Pad Tiere
© 2017 Ciparum LLC
ISBN-10:1-63589-344-5
ISBN-13:978-1-63589-344-1

Coloring Pages for Kids

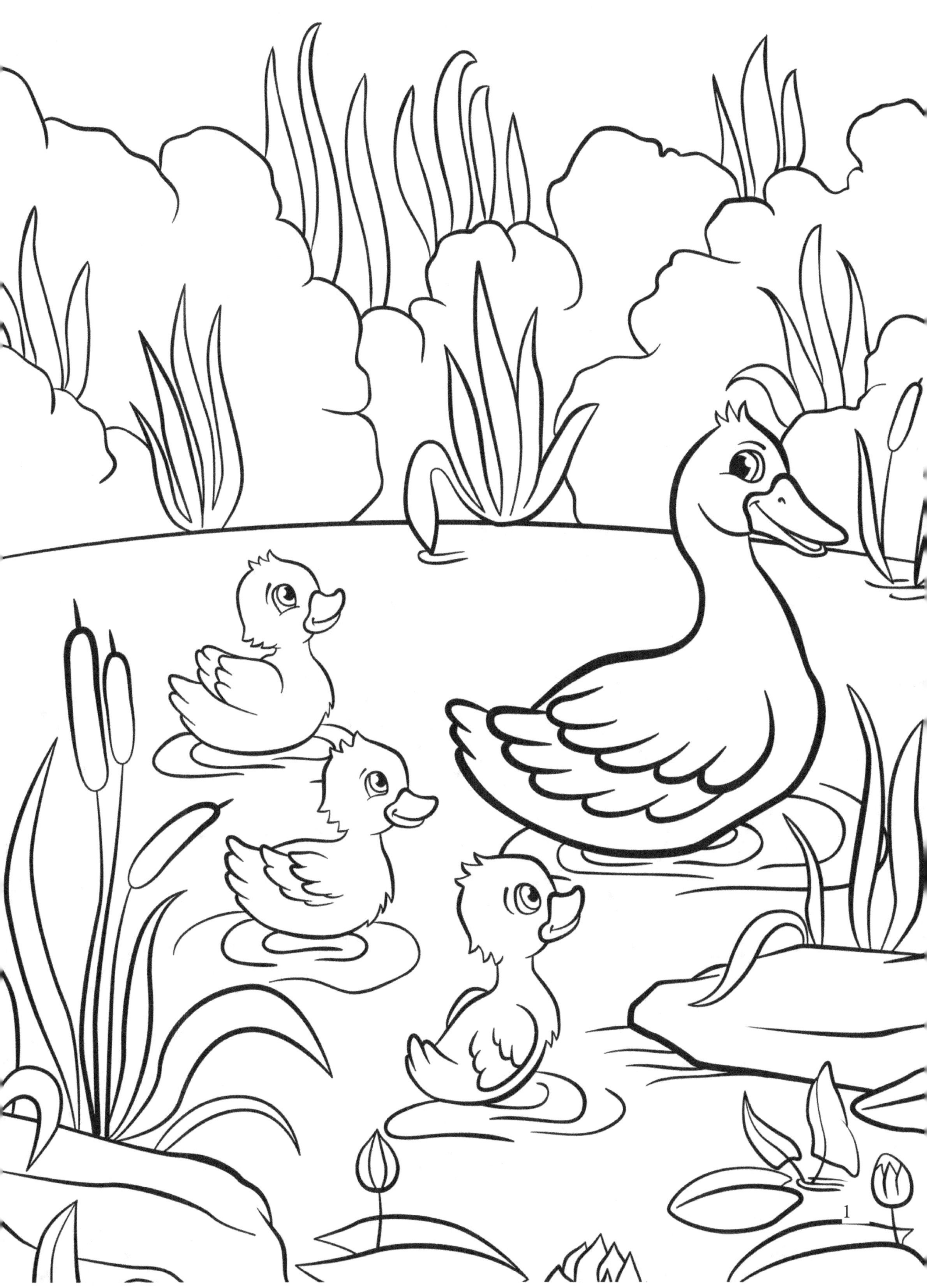

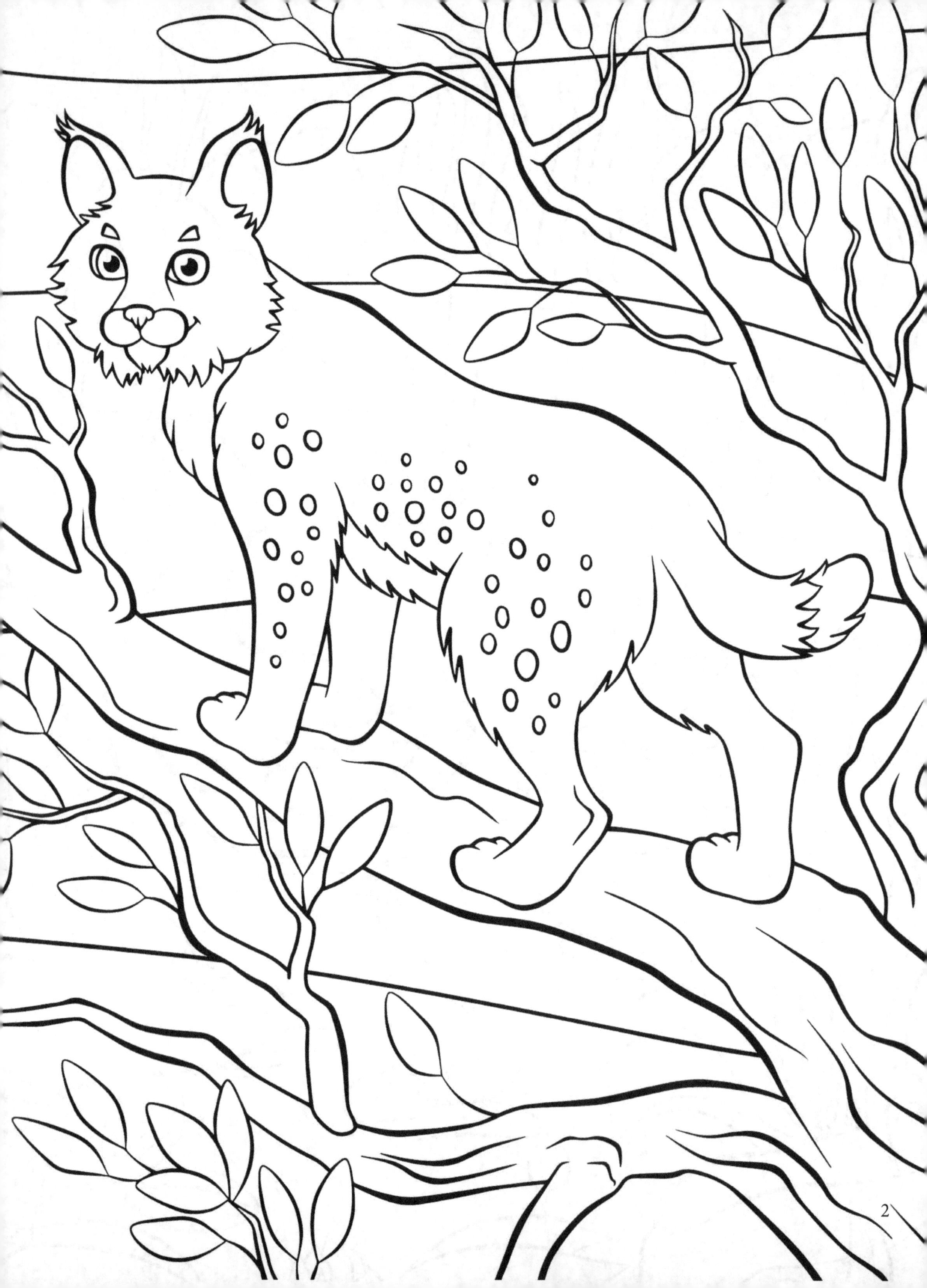

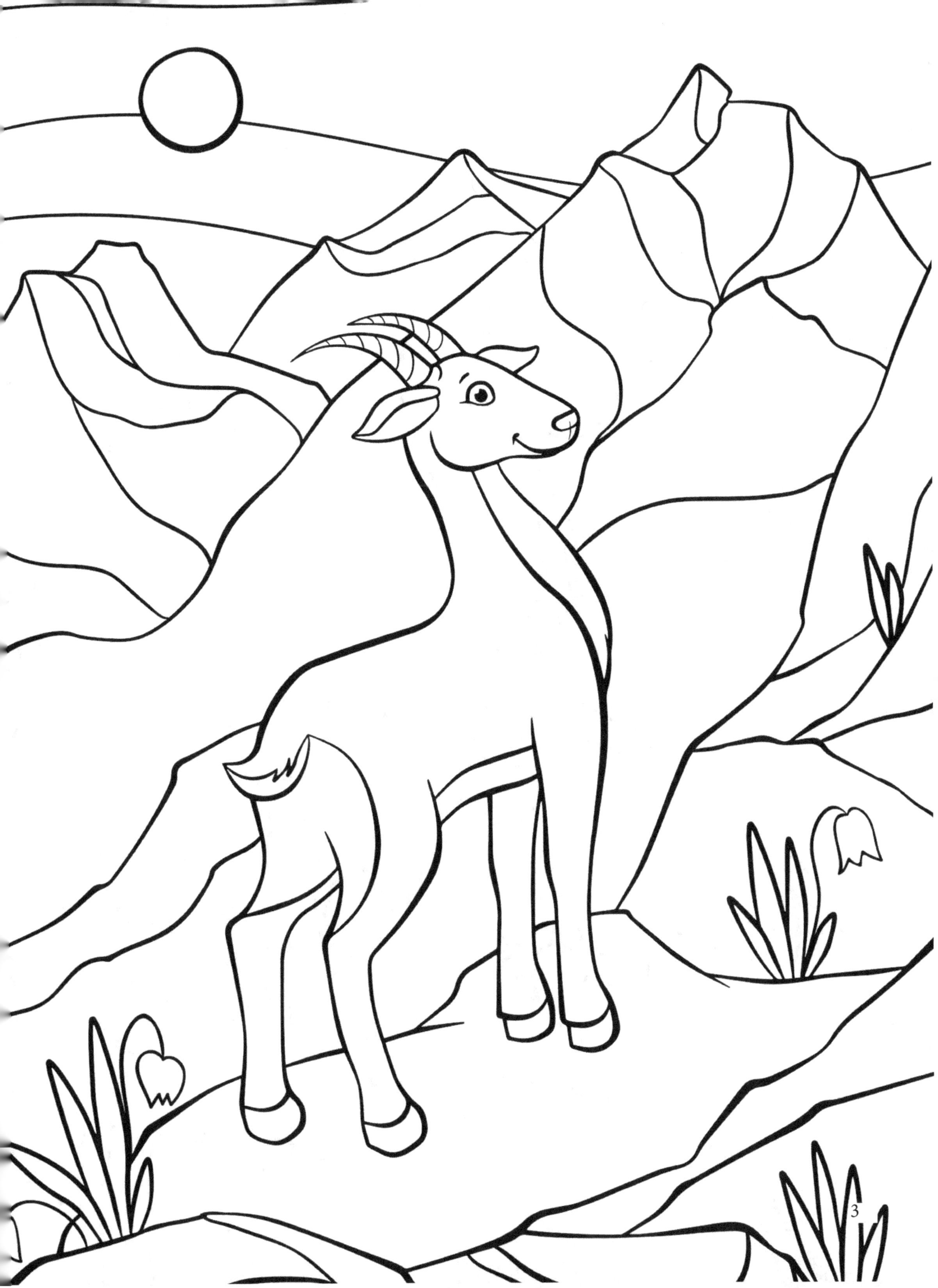

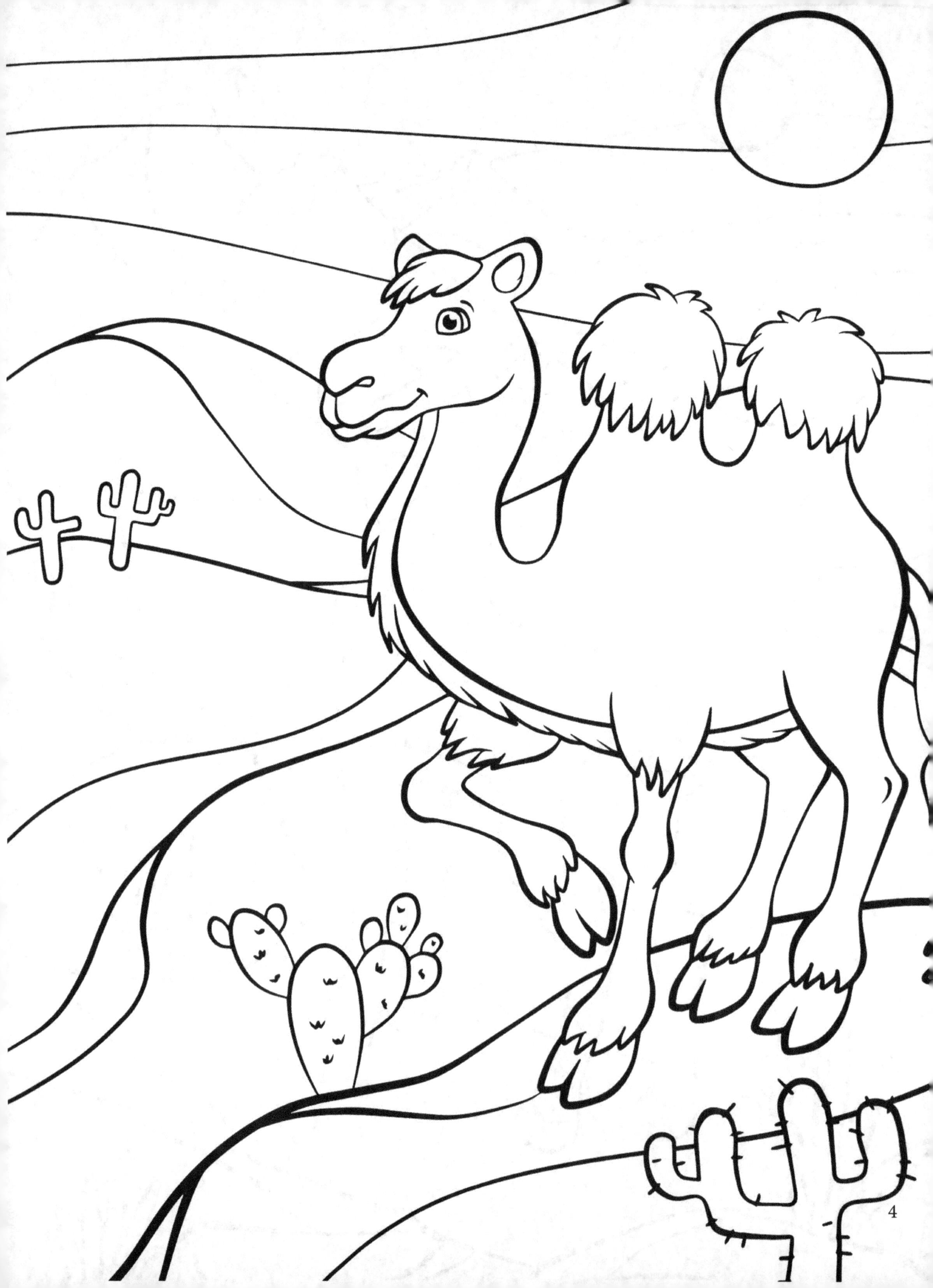

4

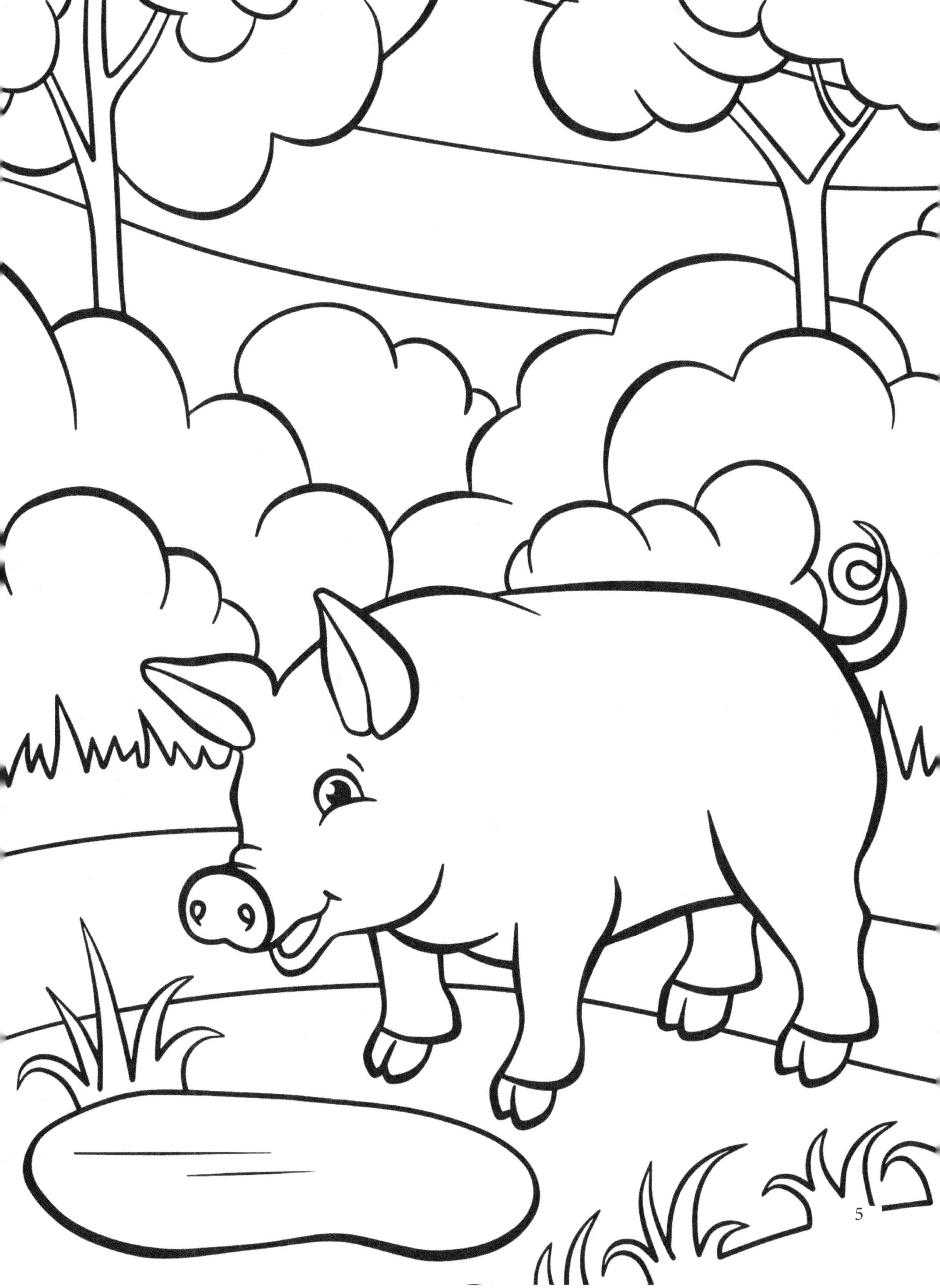

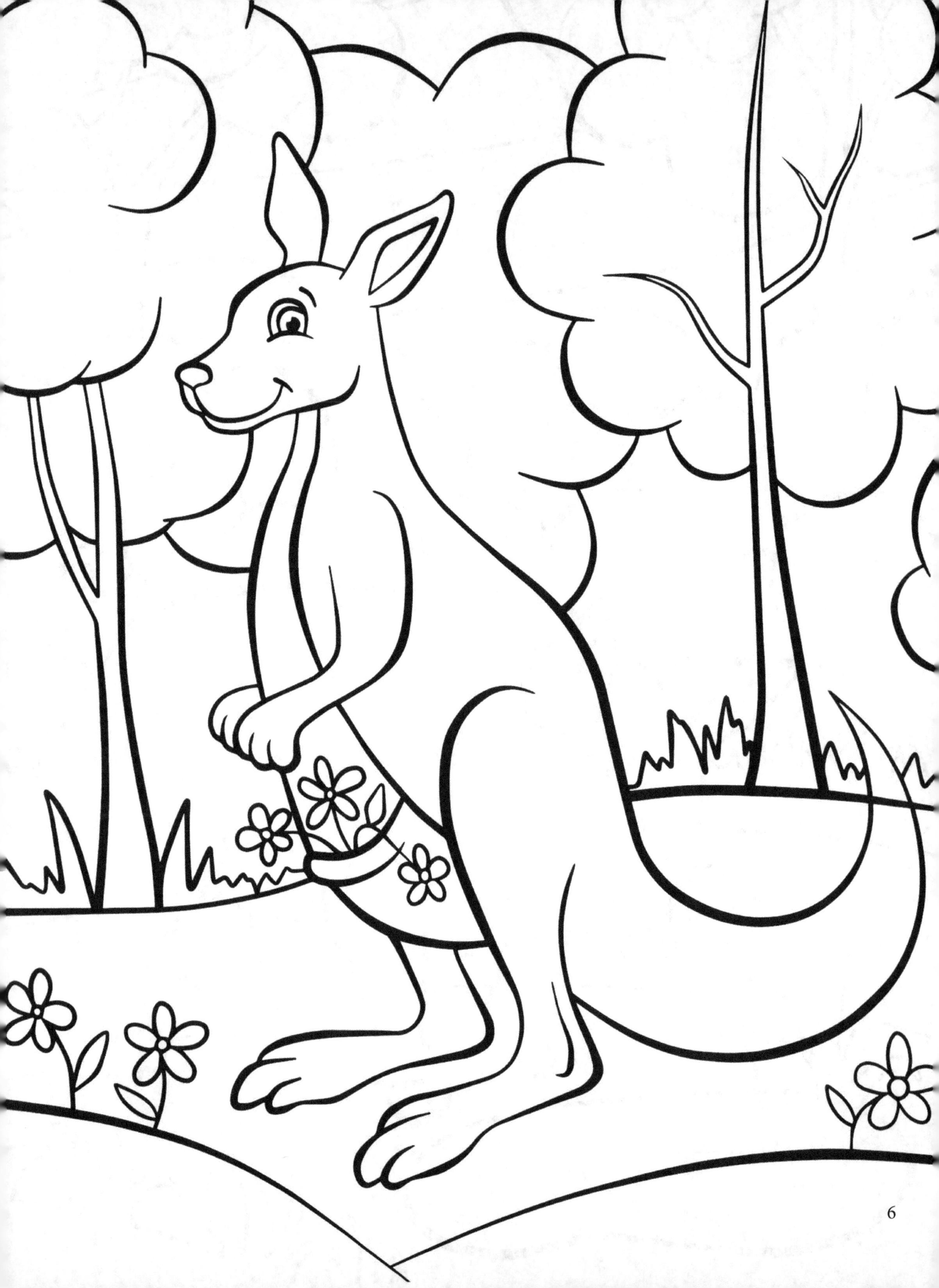

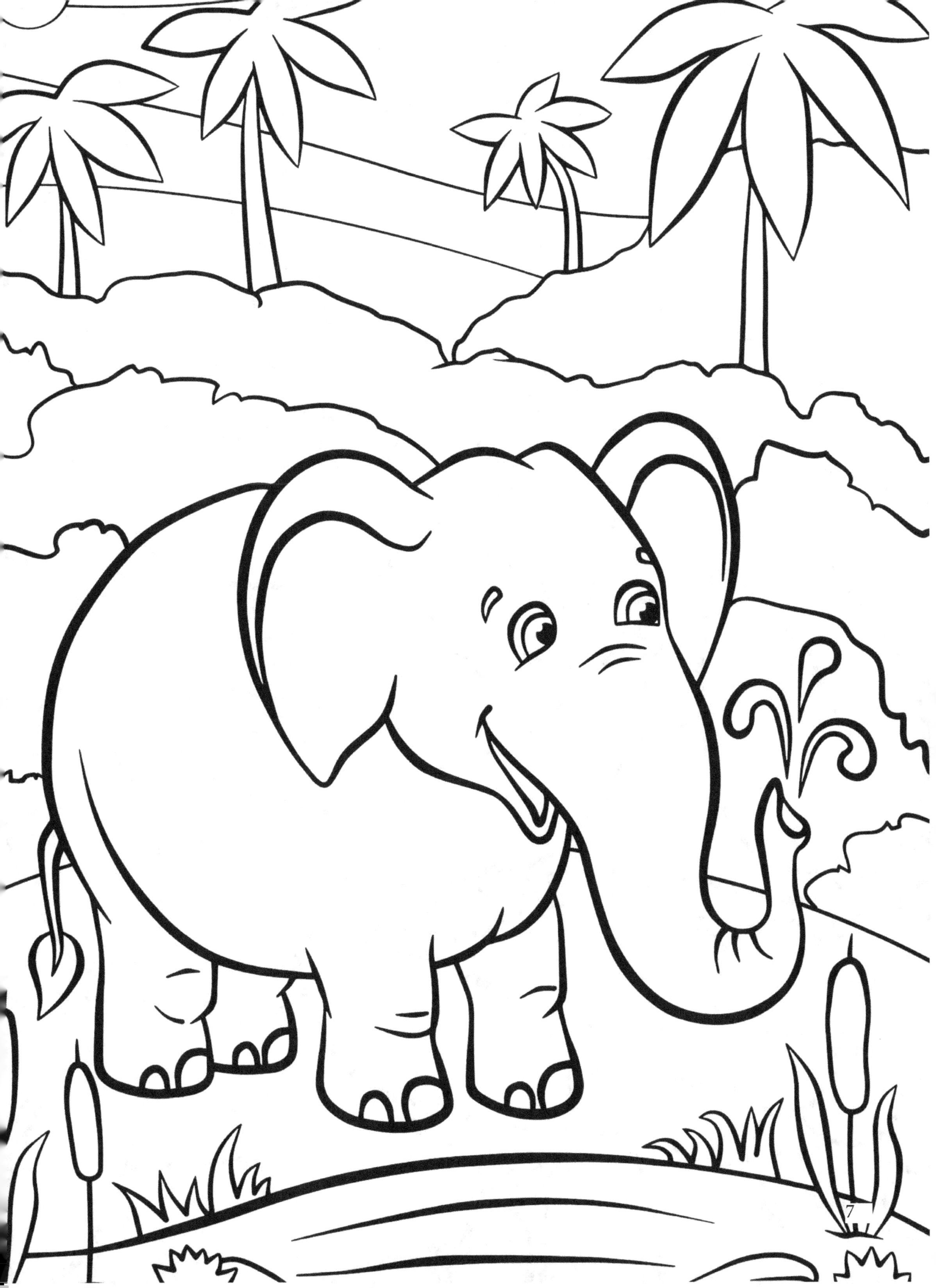

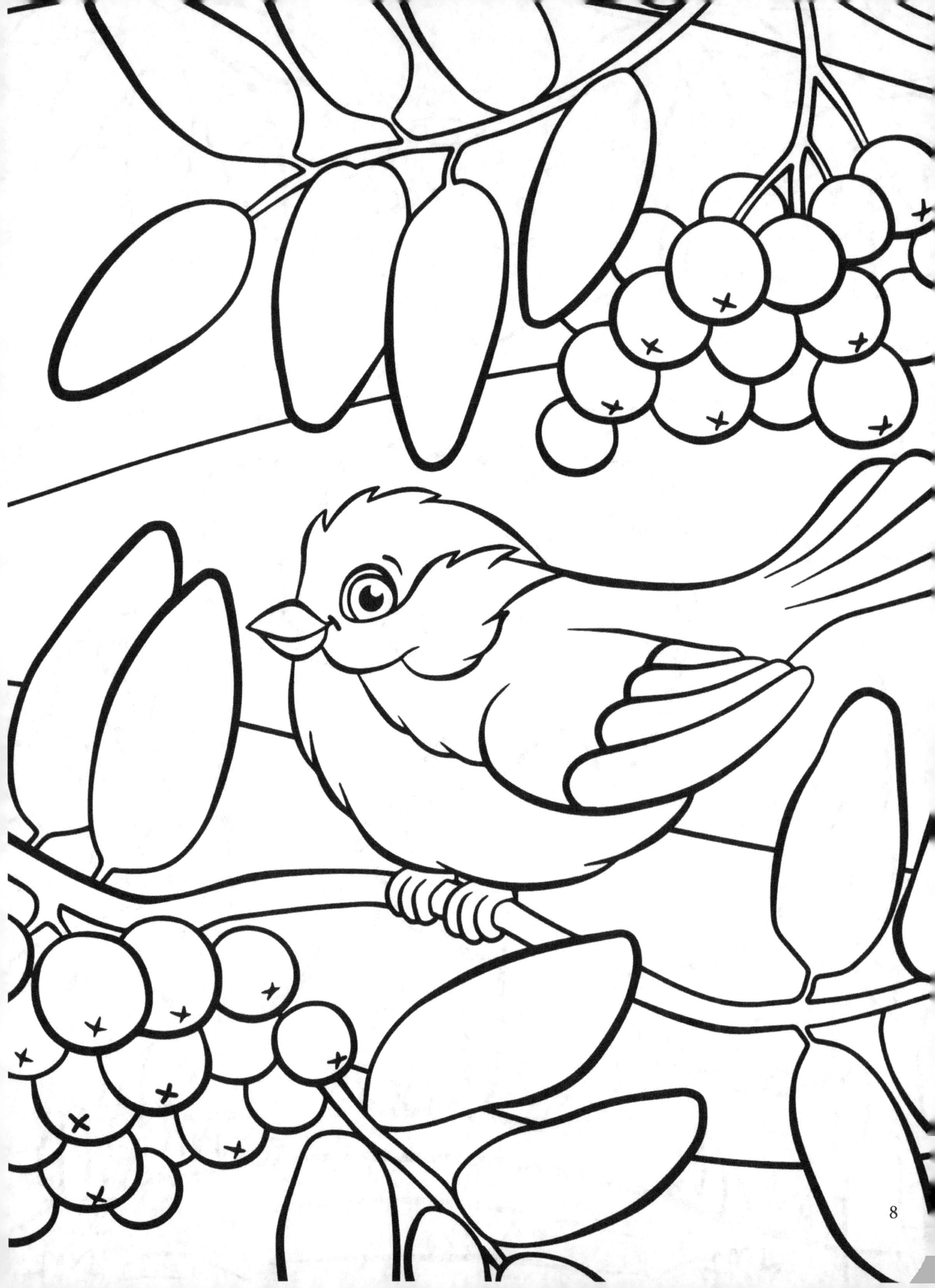

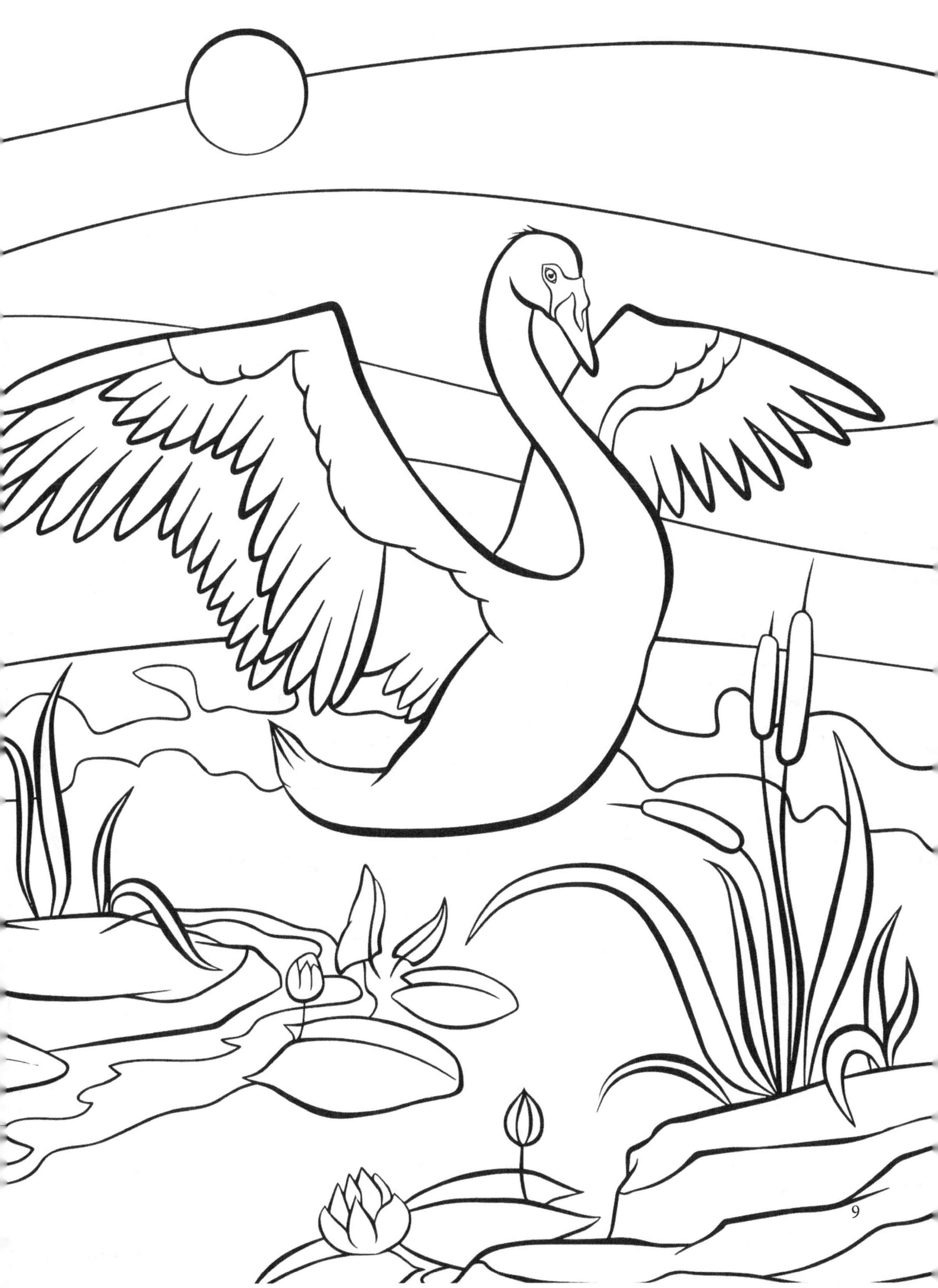

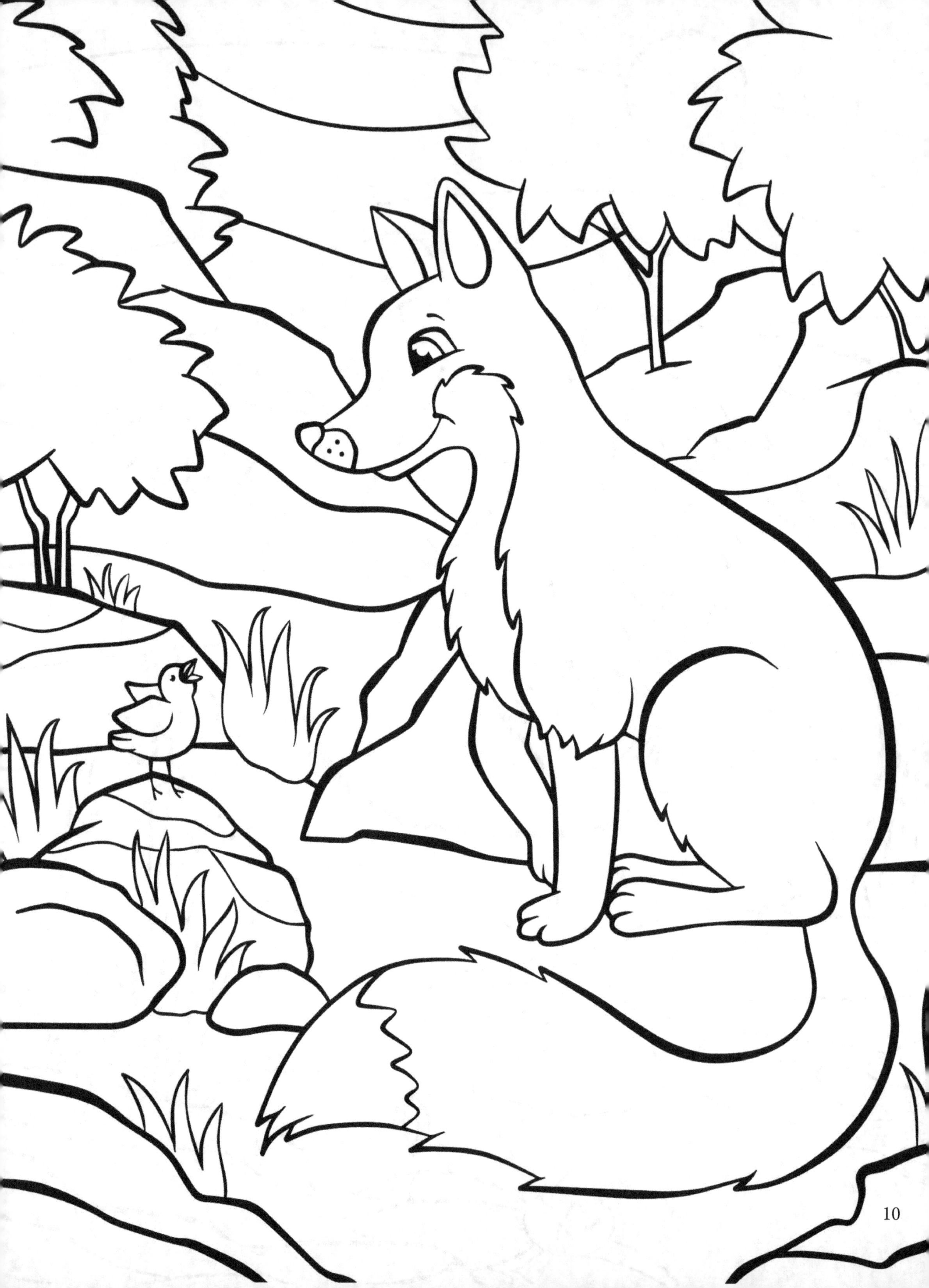

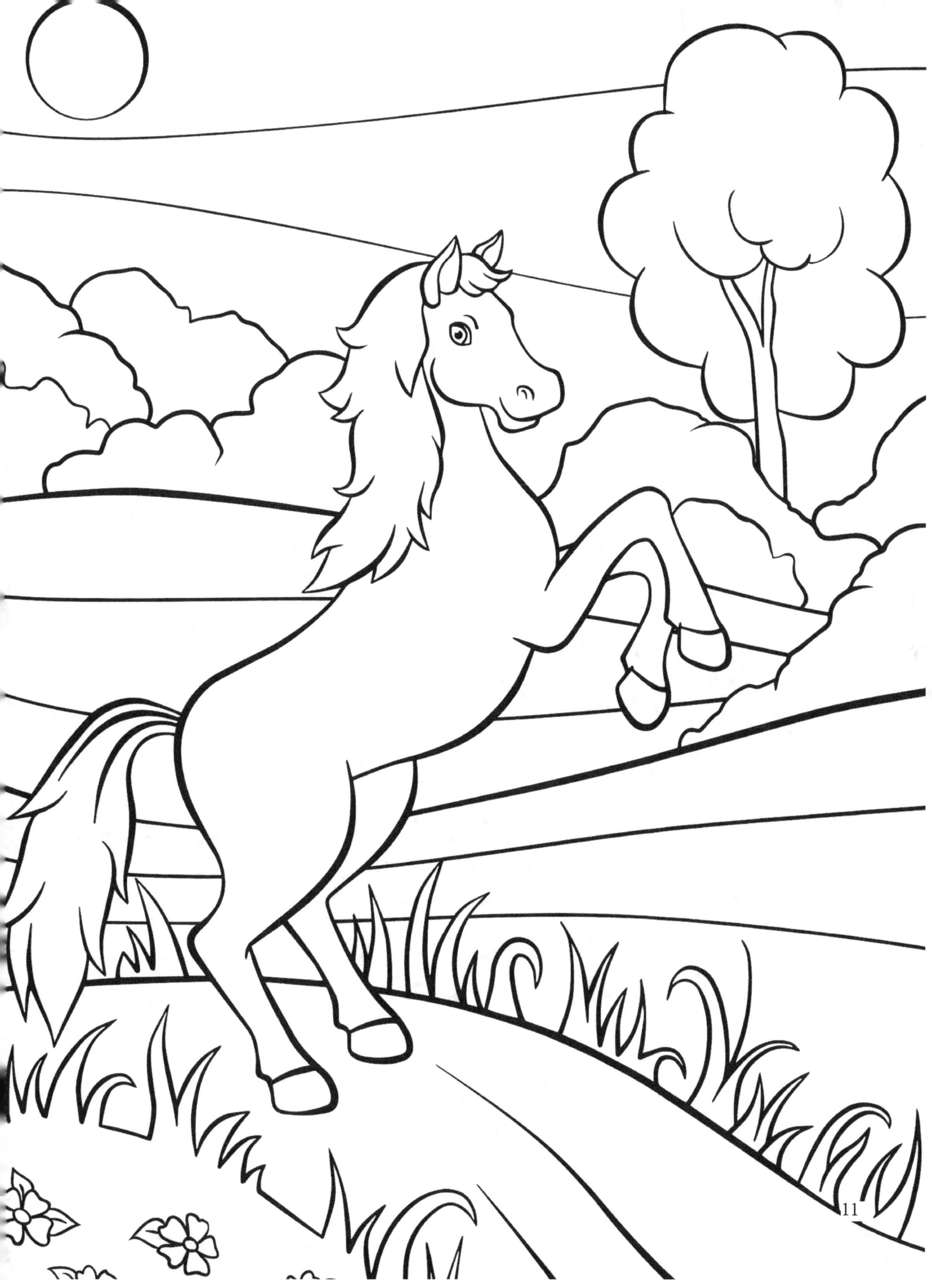

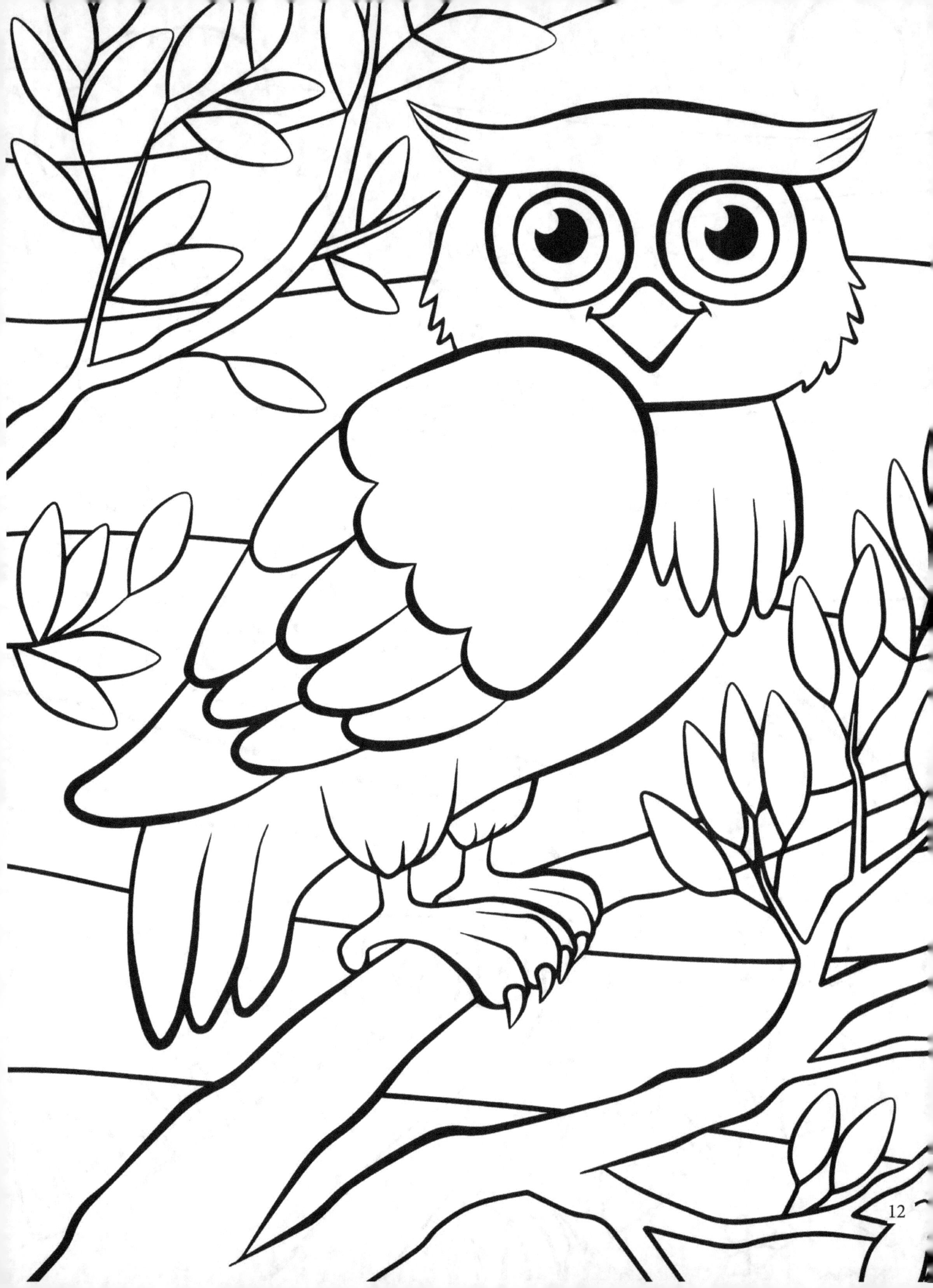

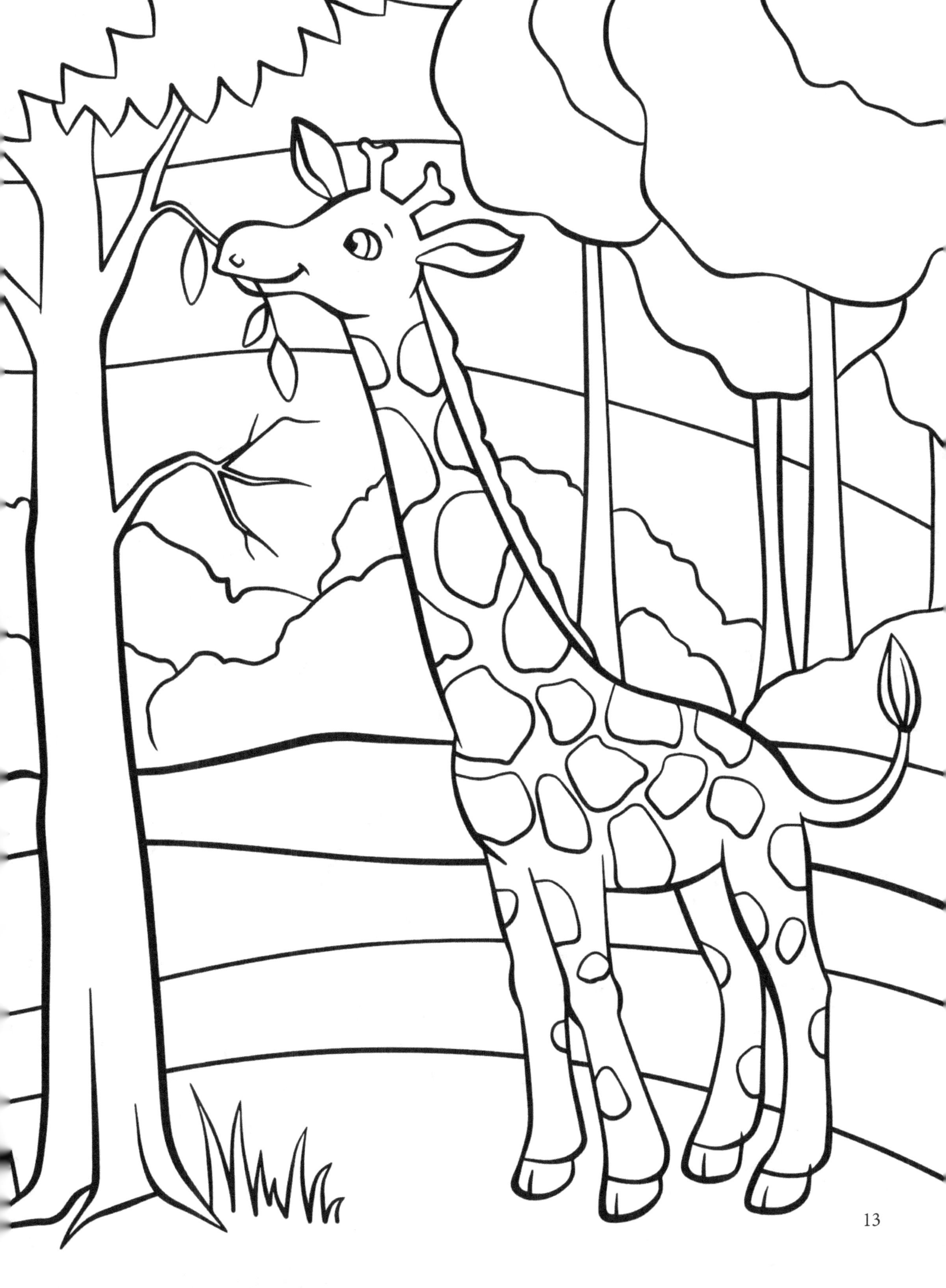

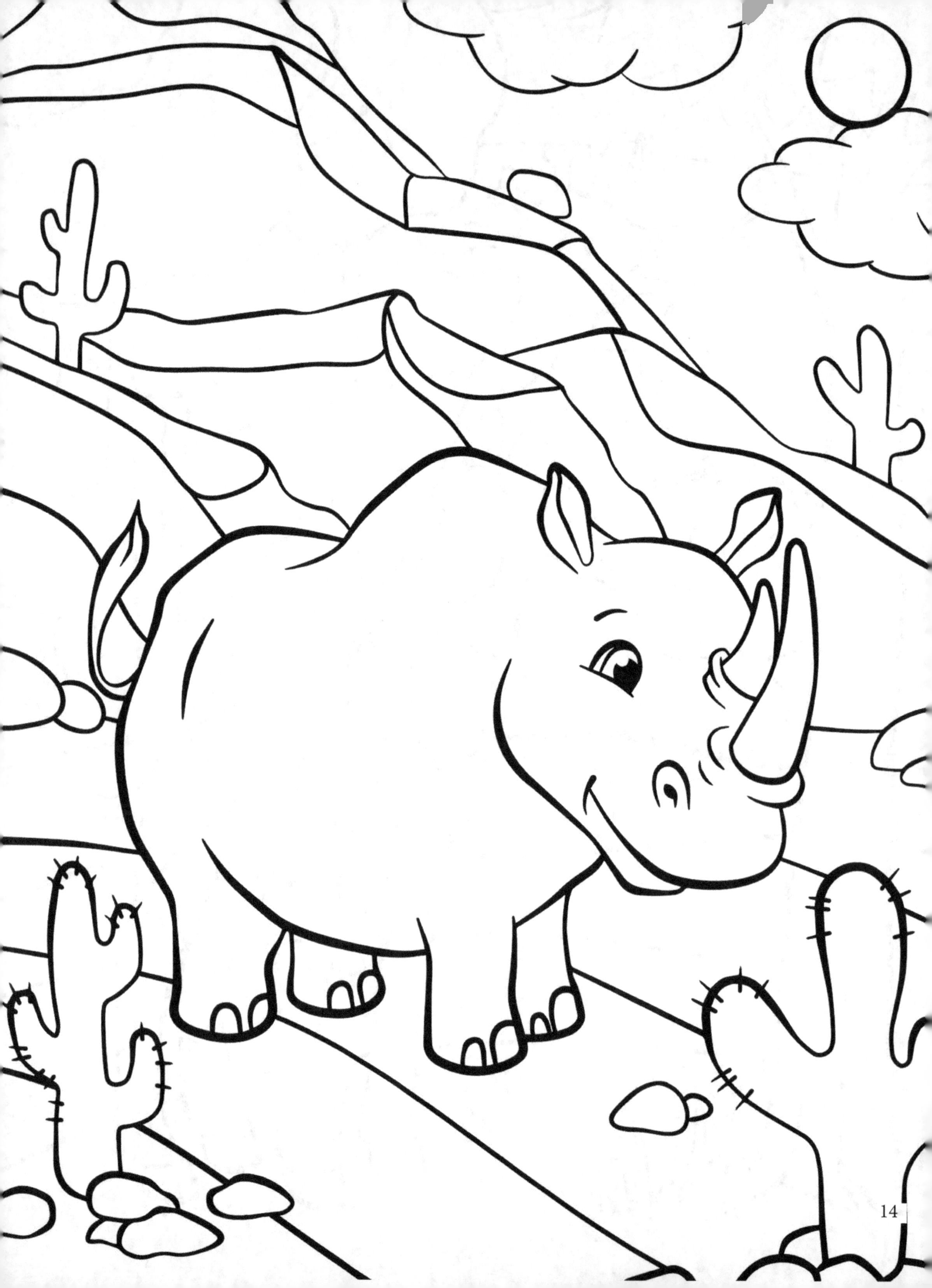

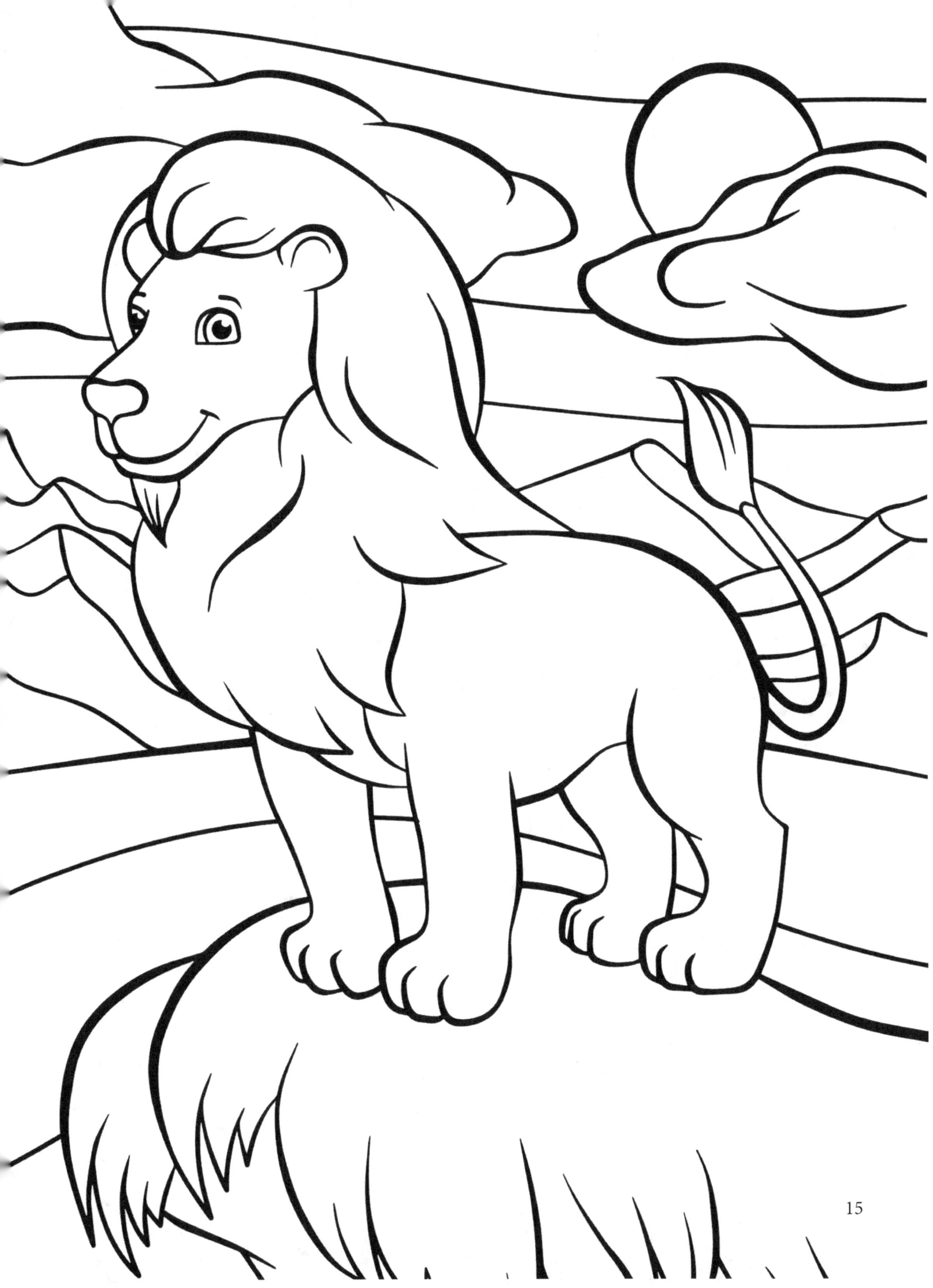

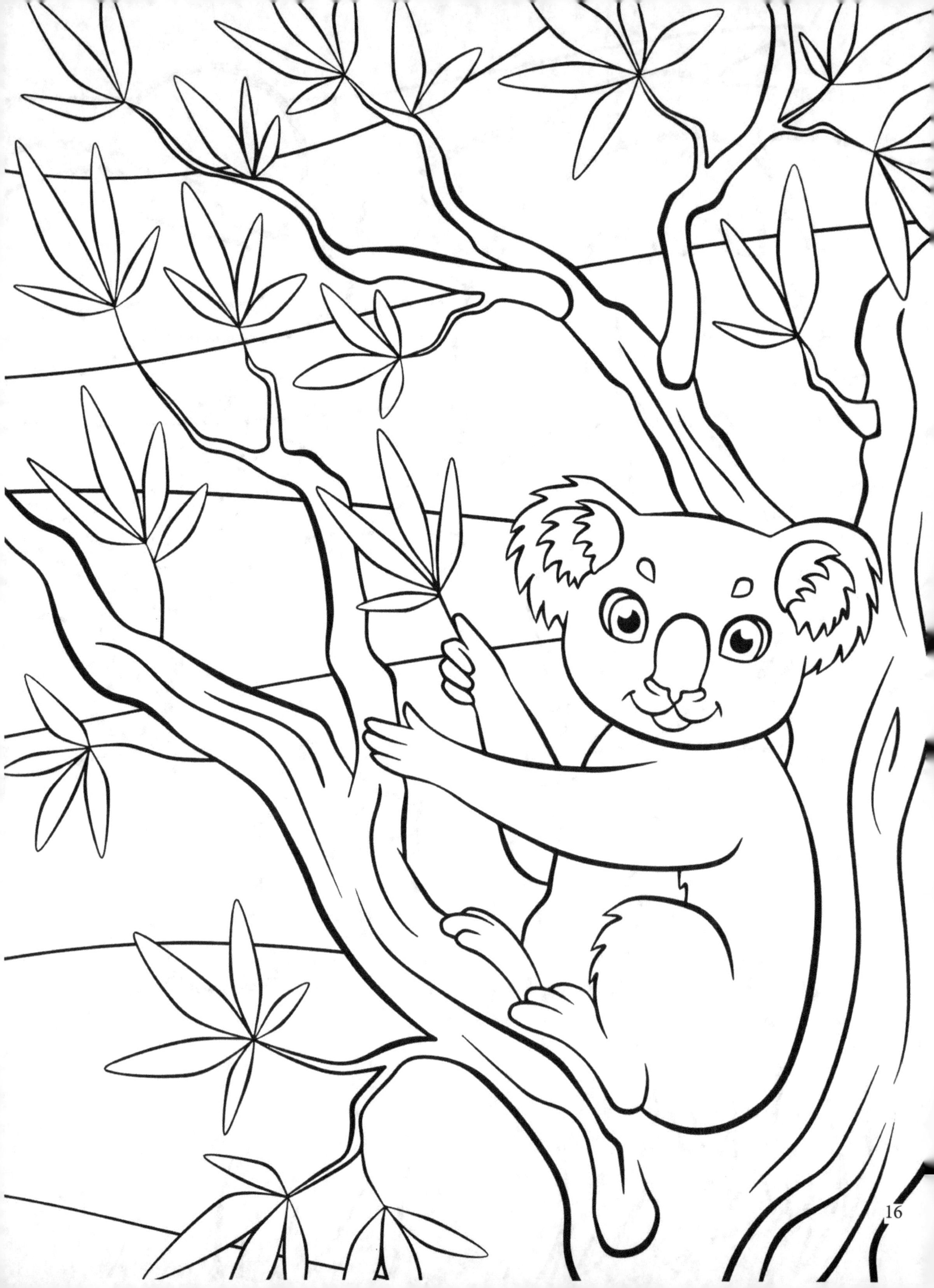

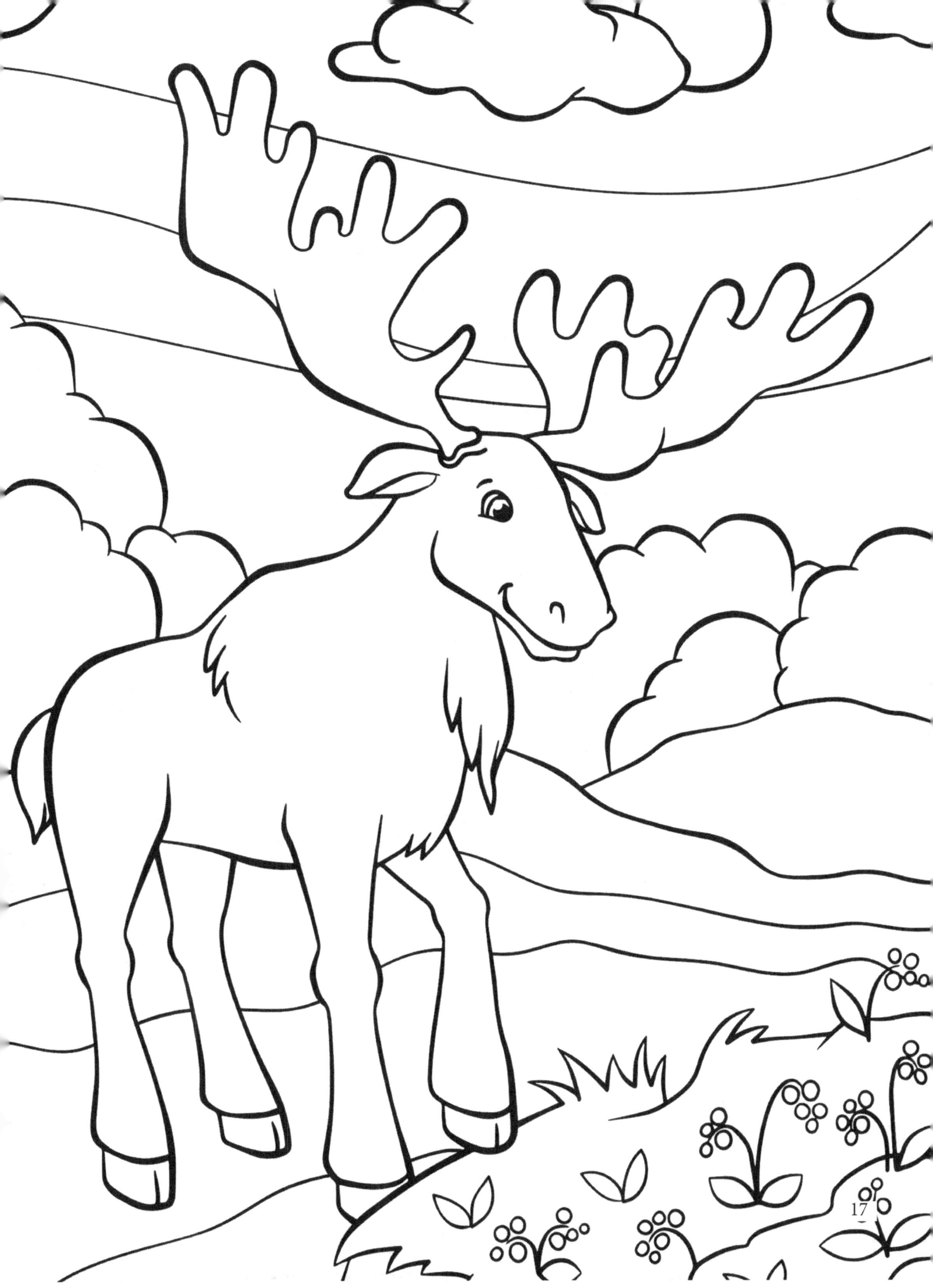

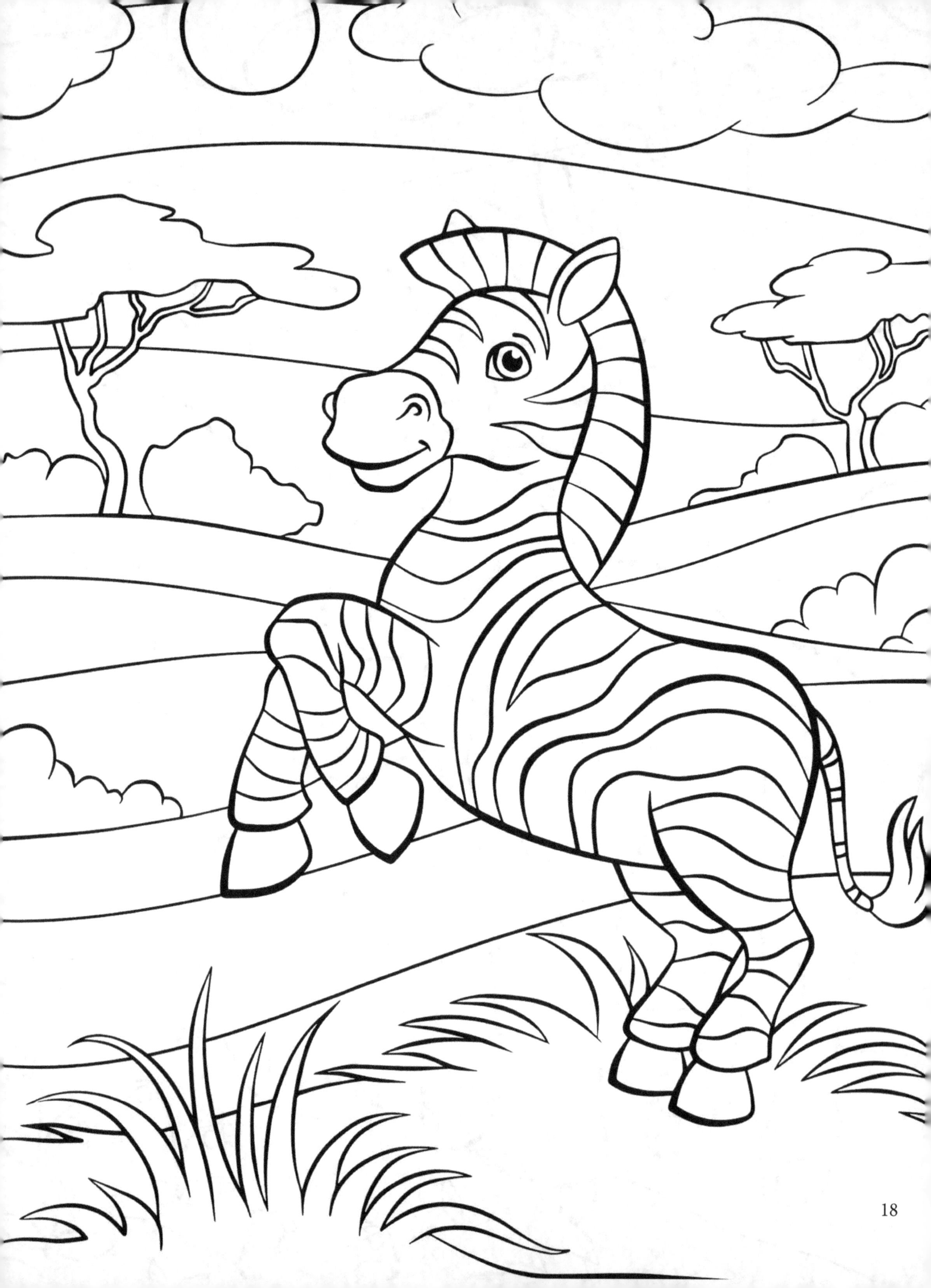

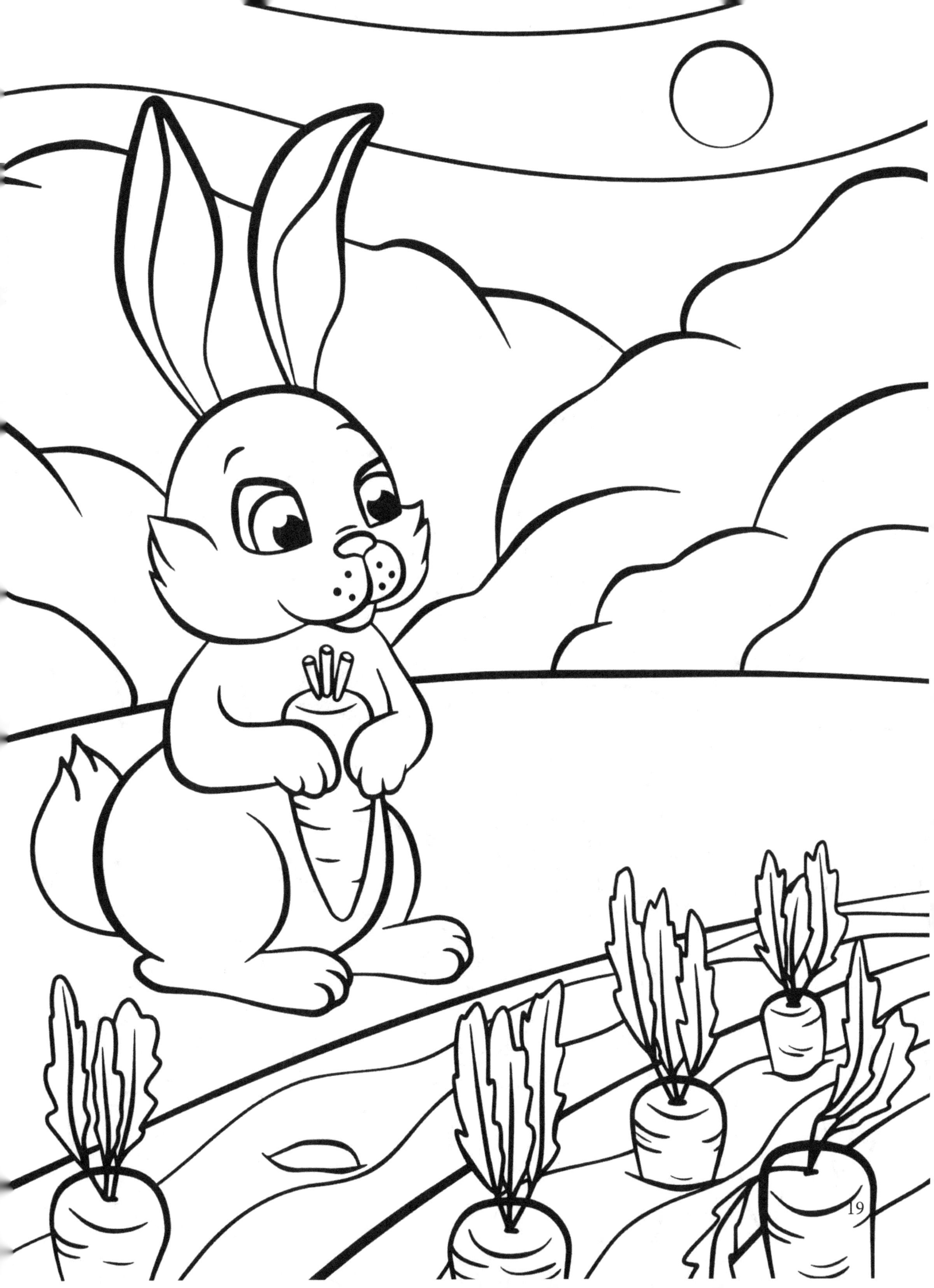

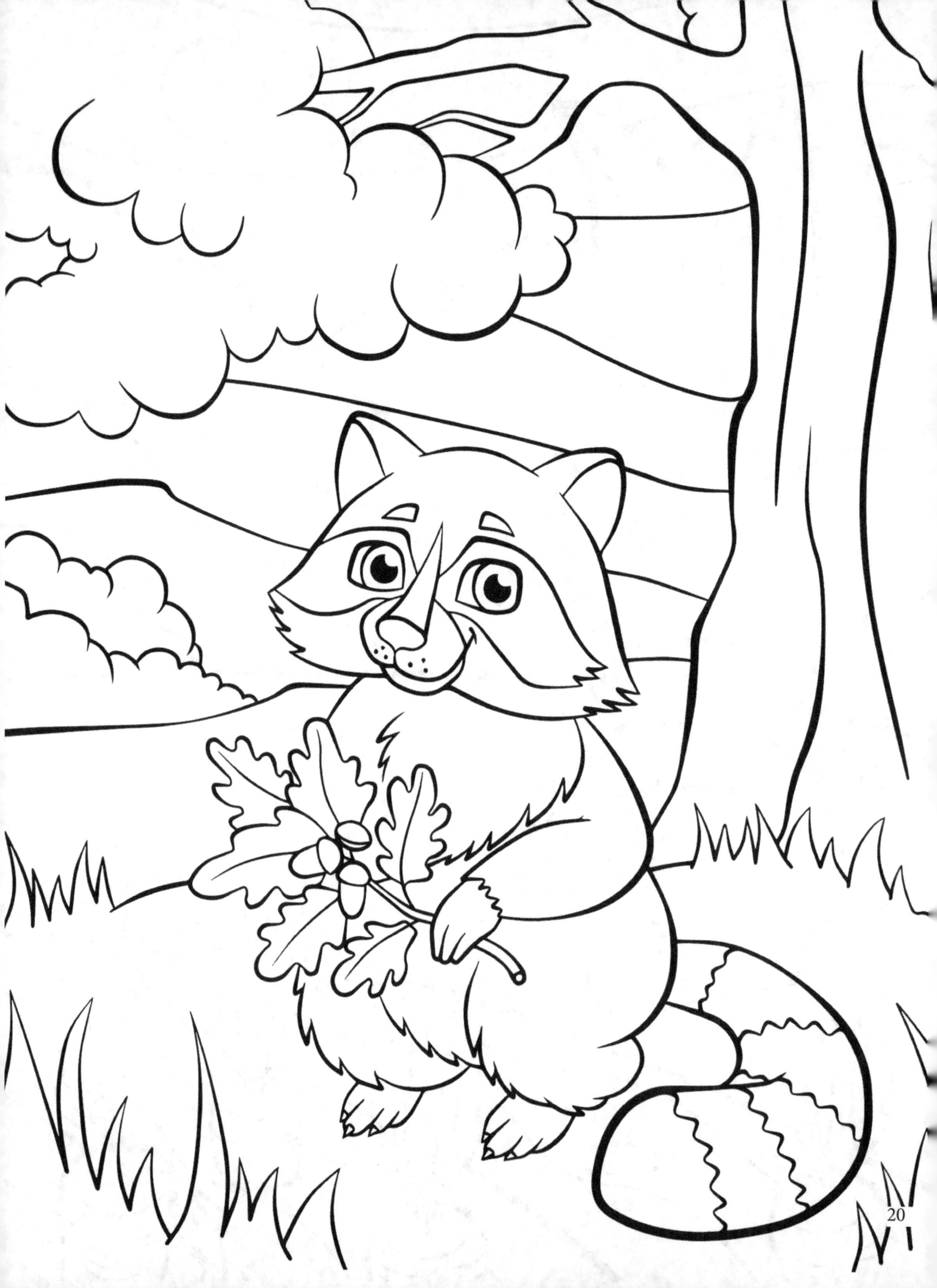

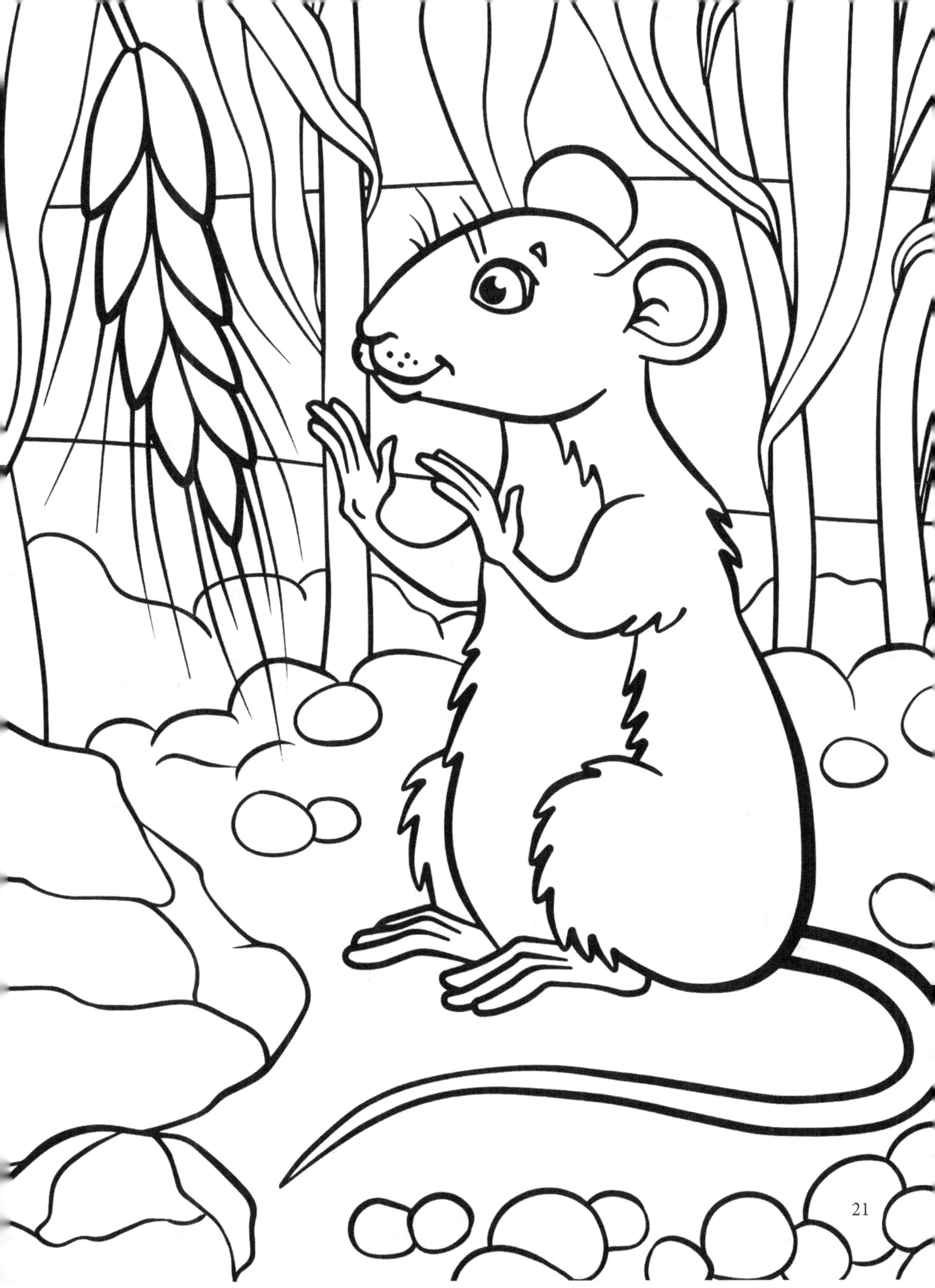

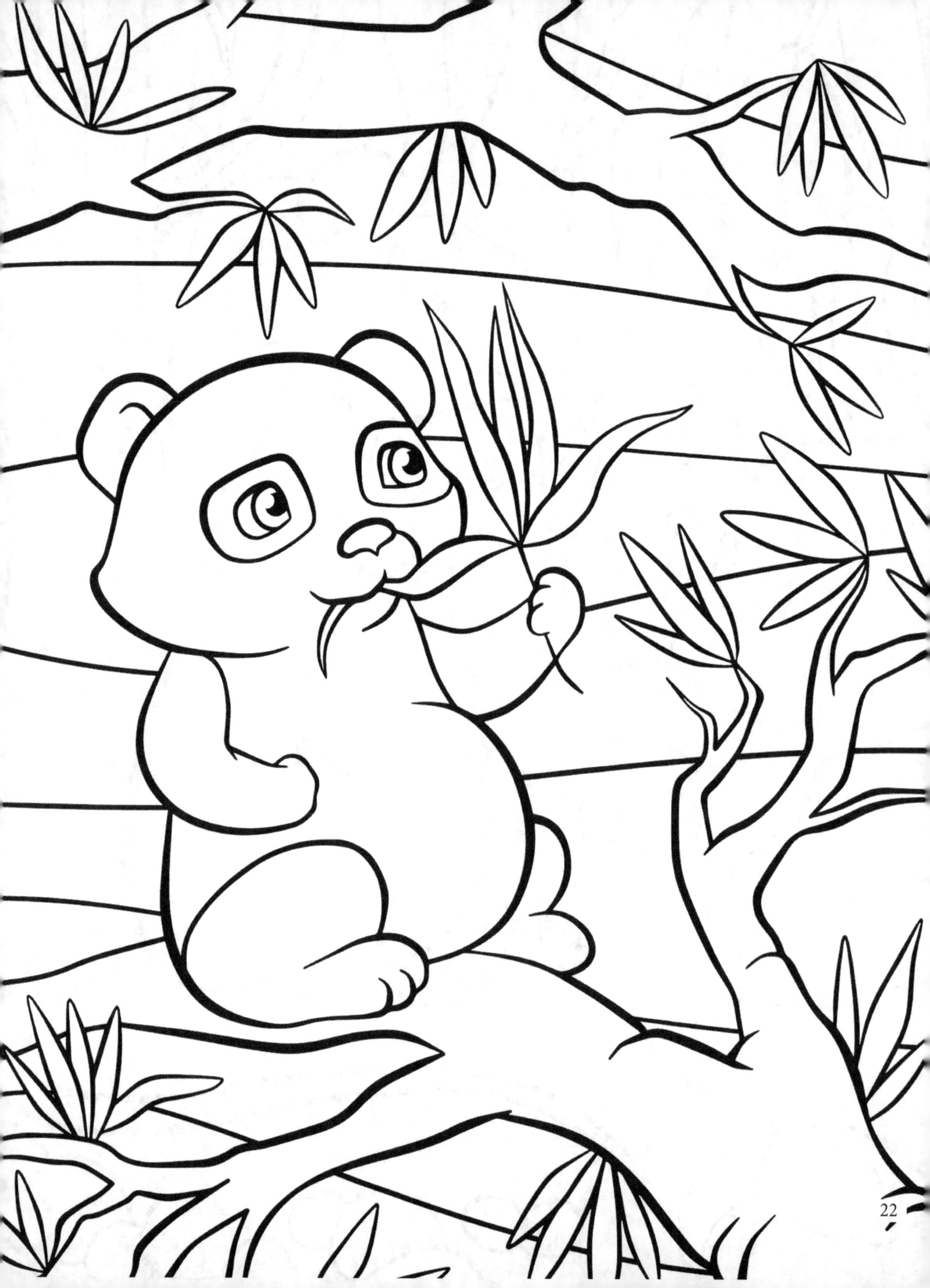

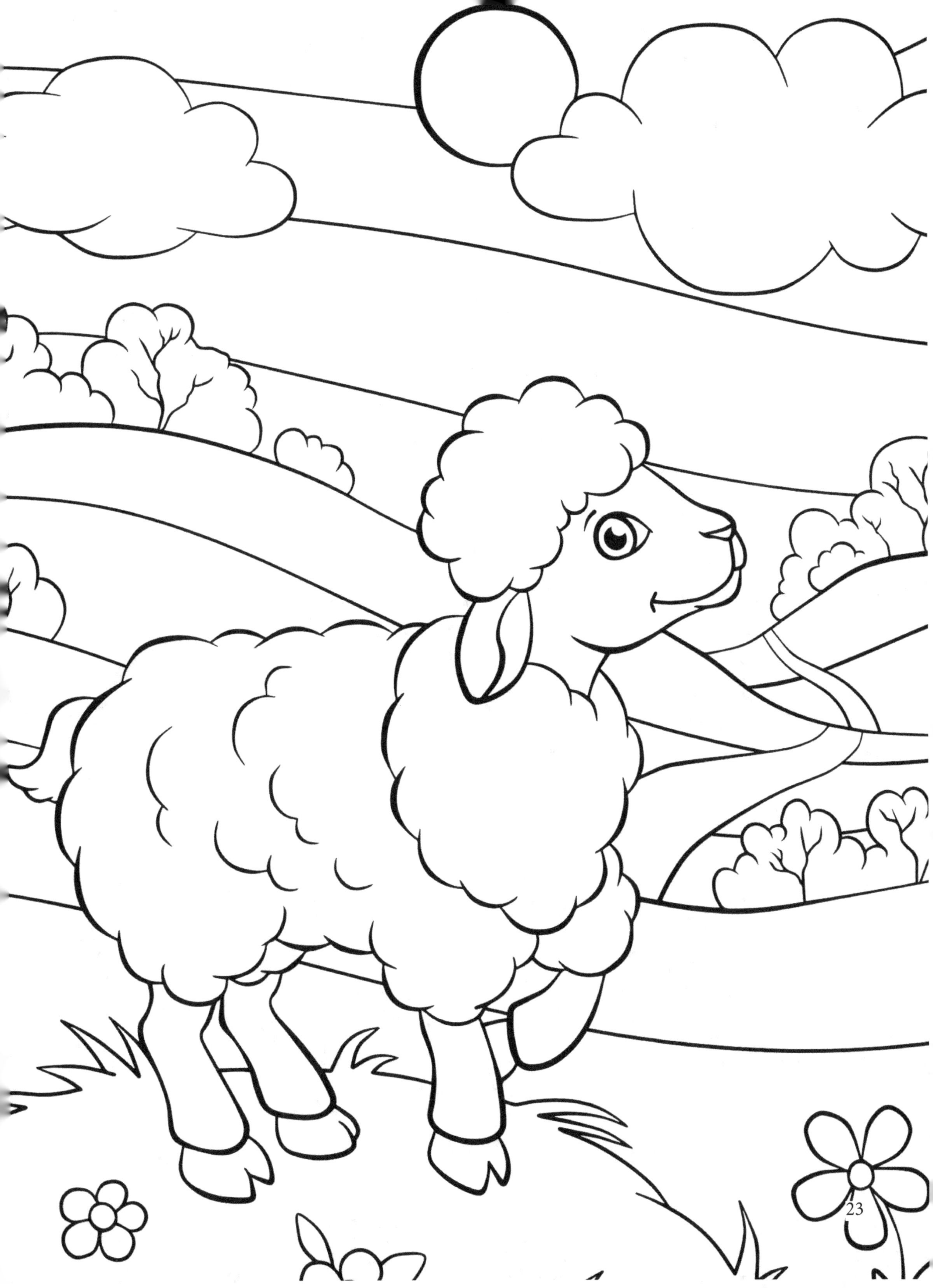

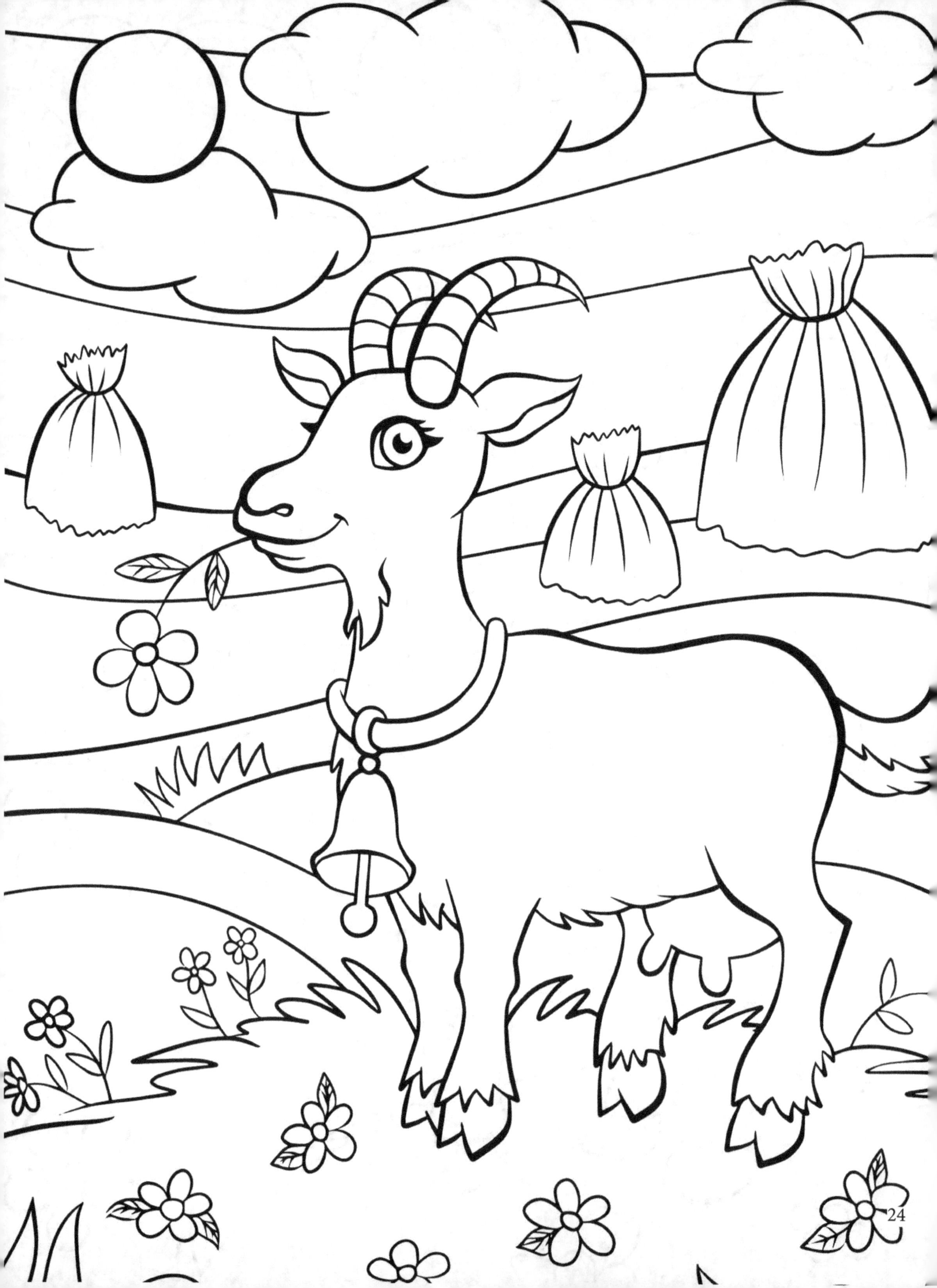

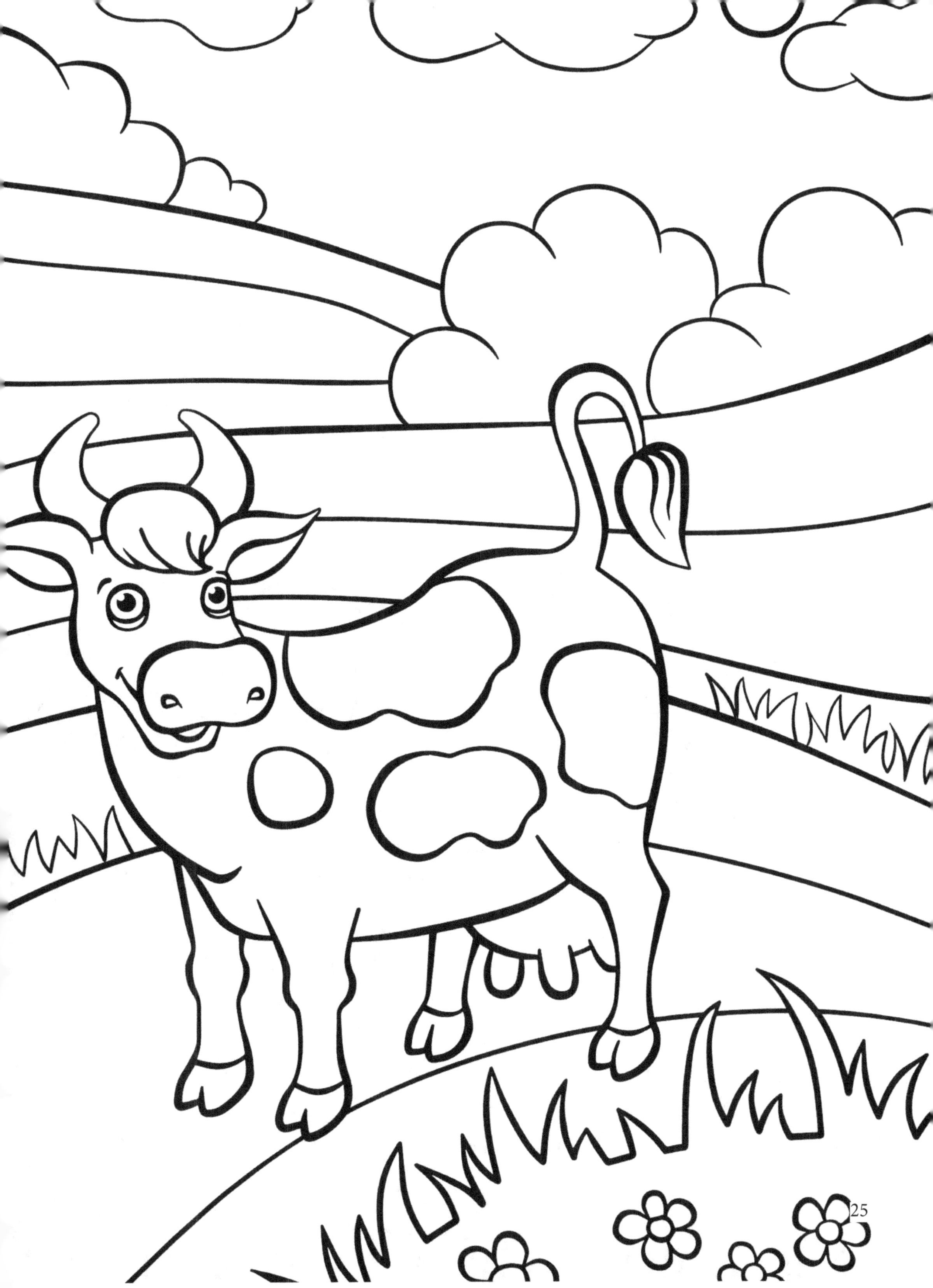

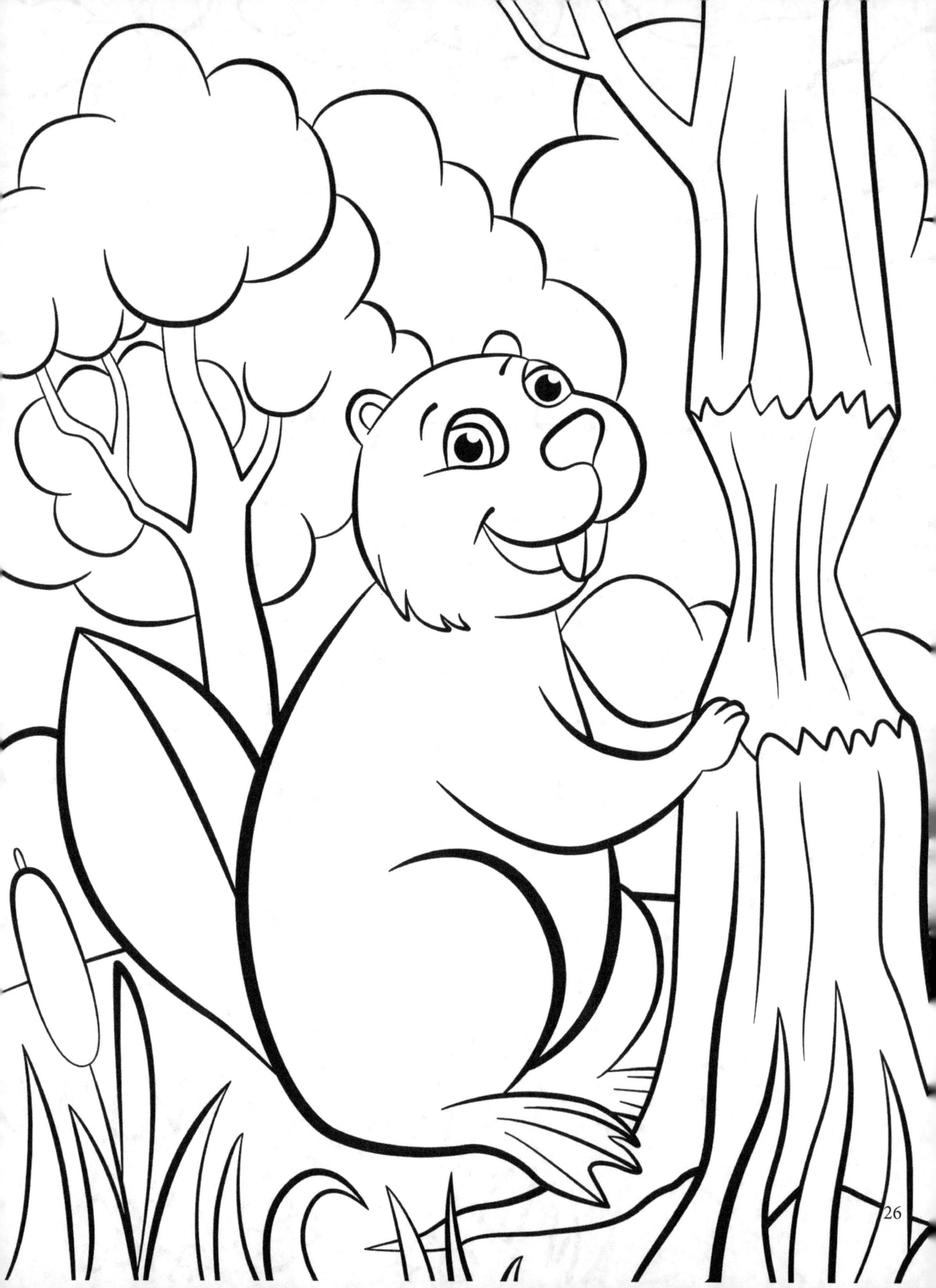

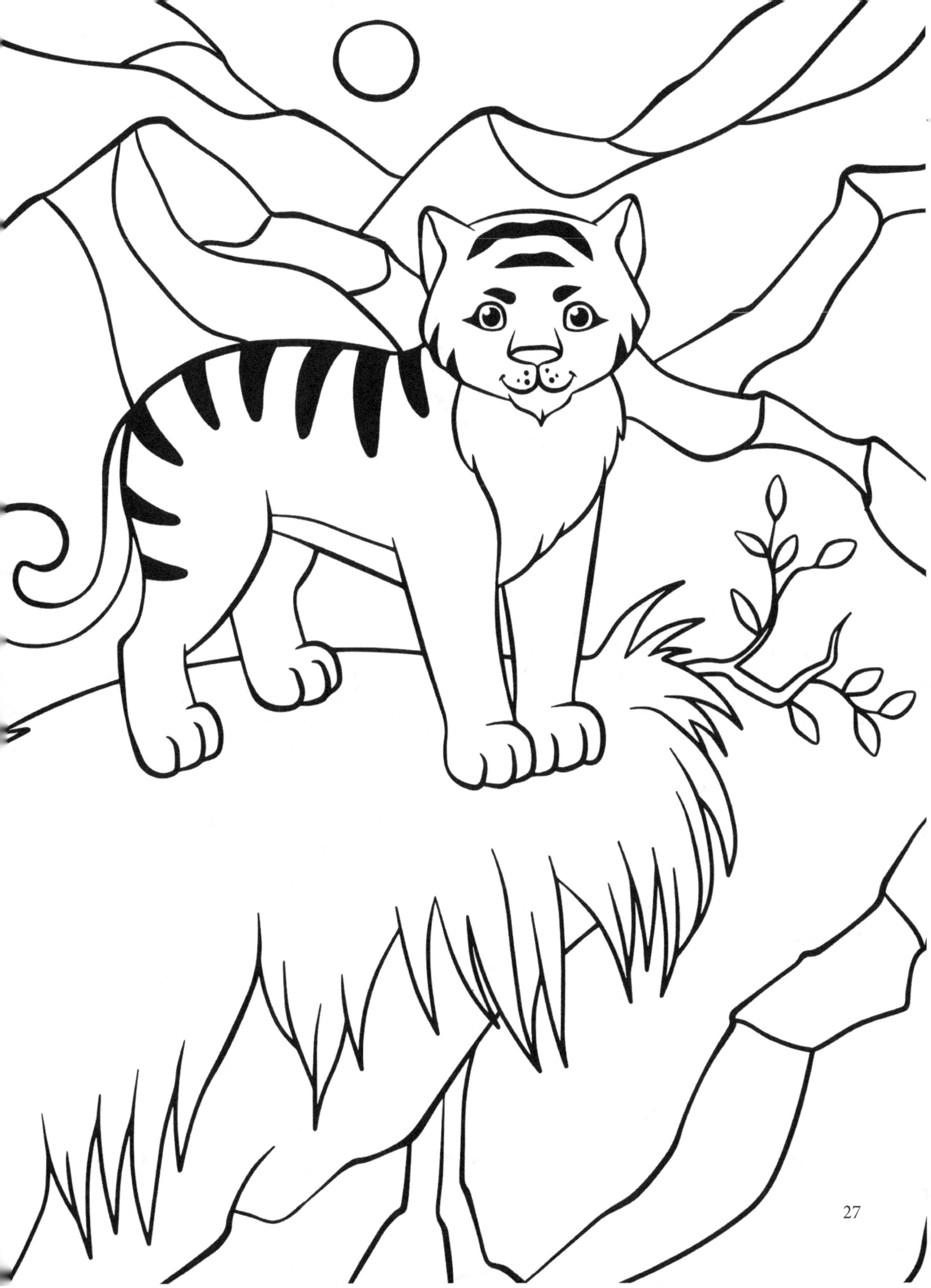

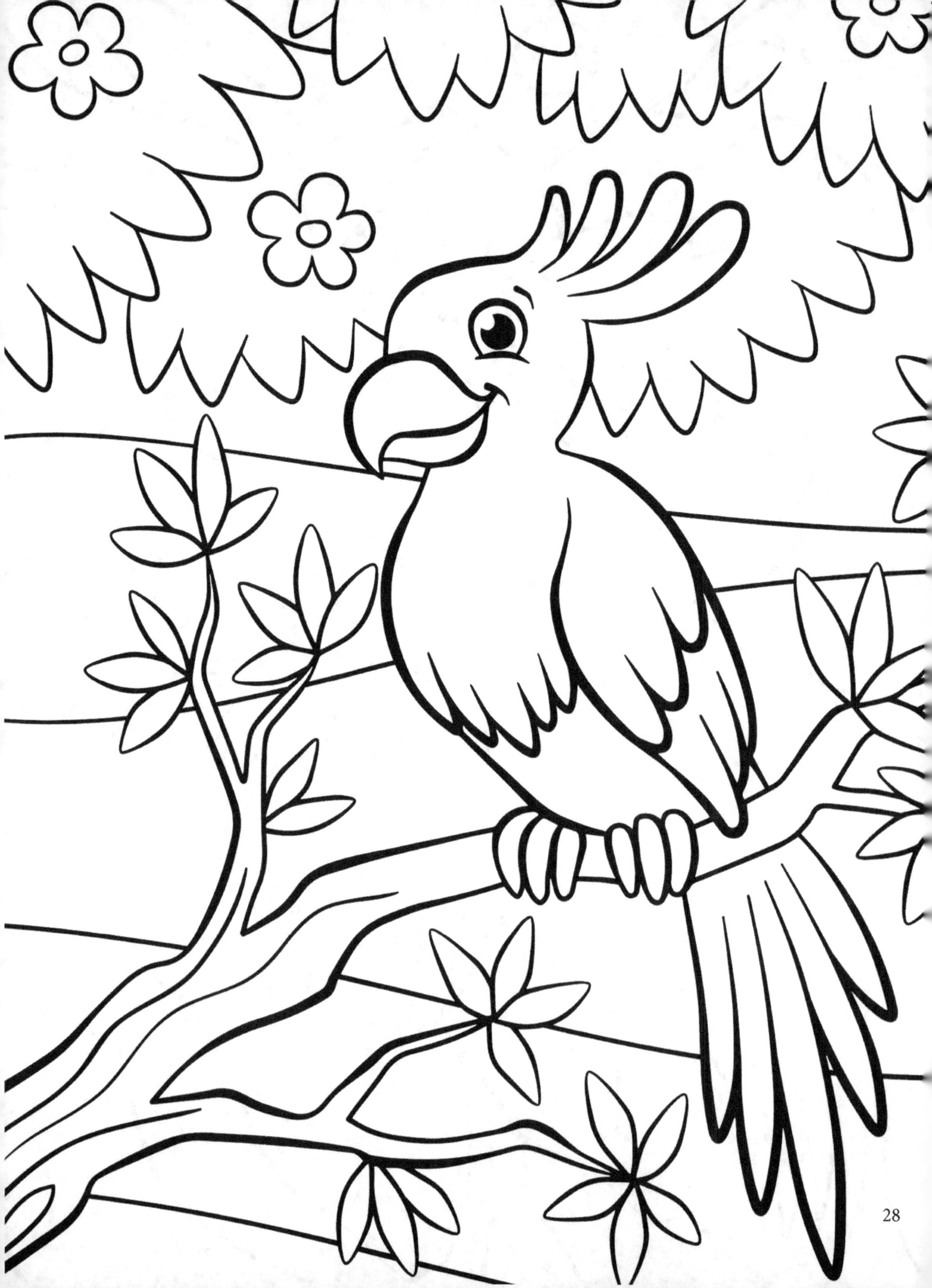

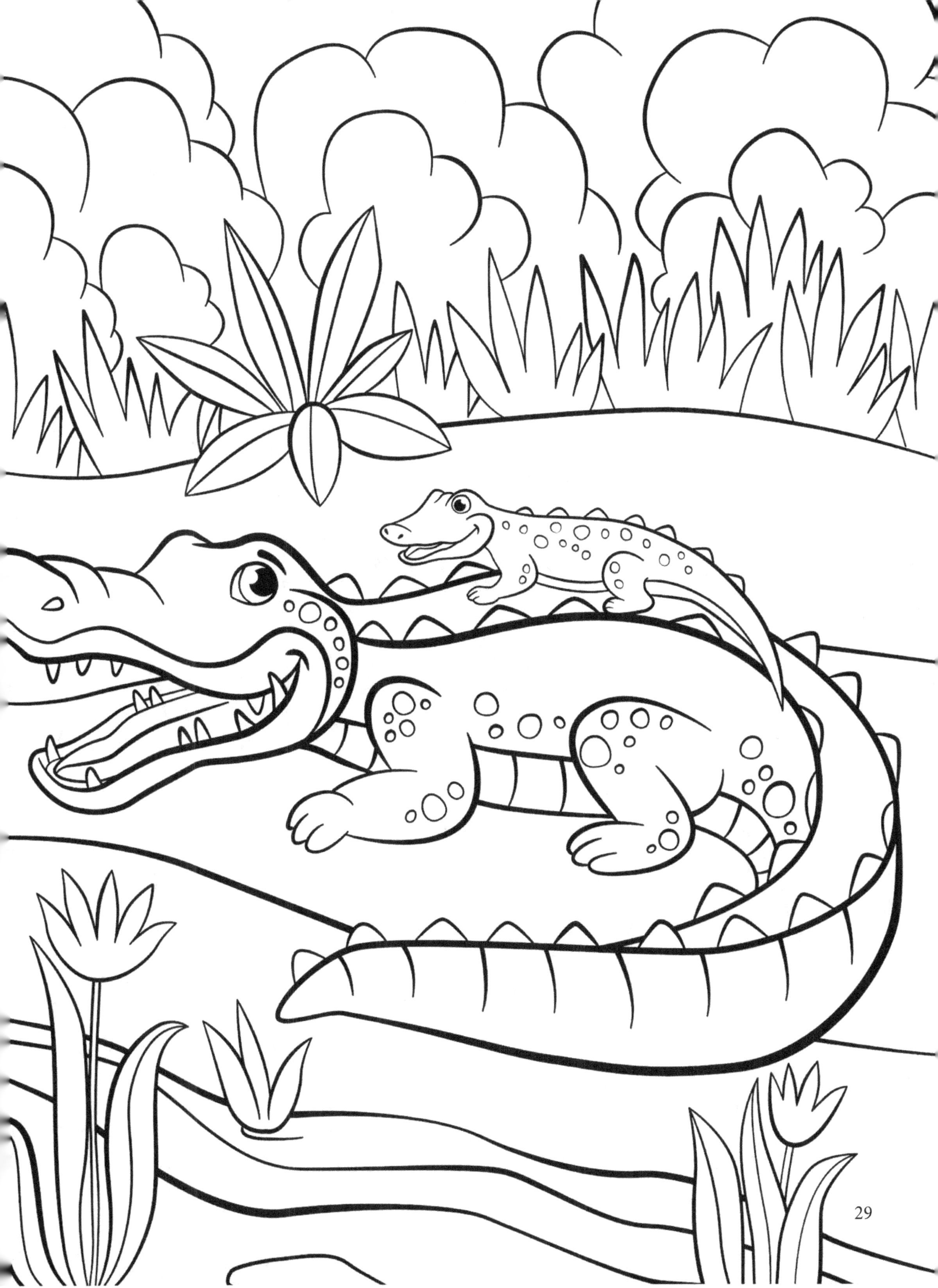

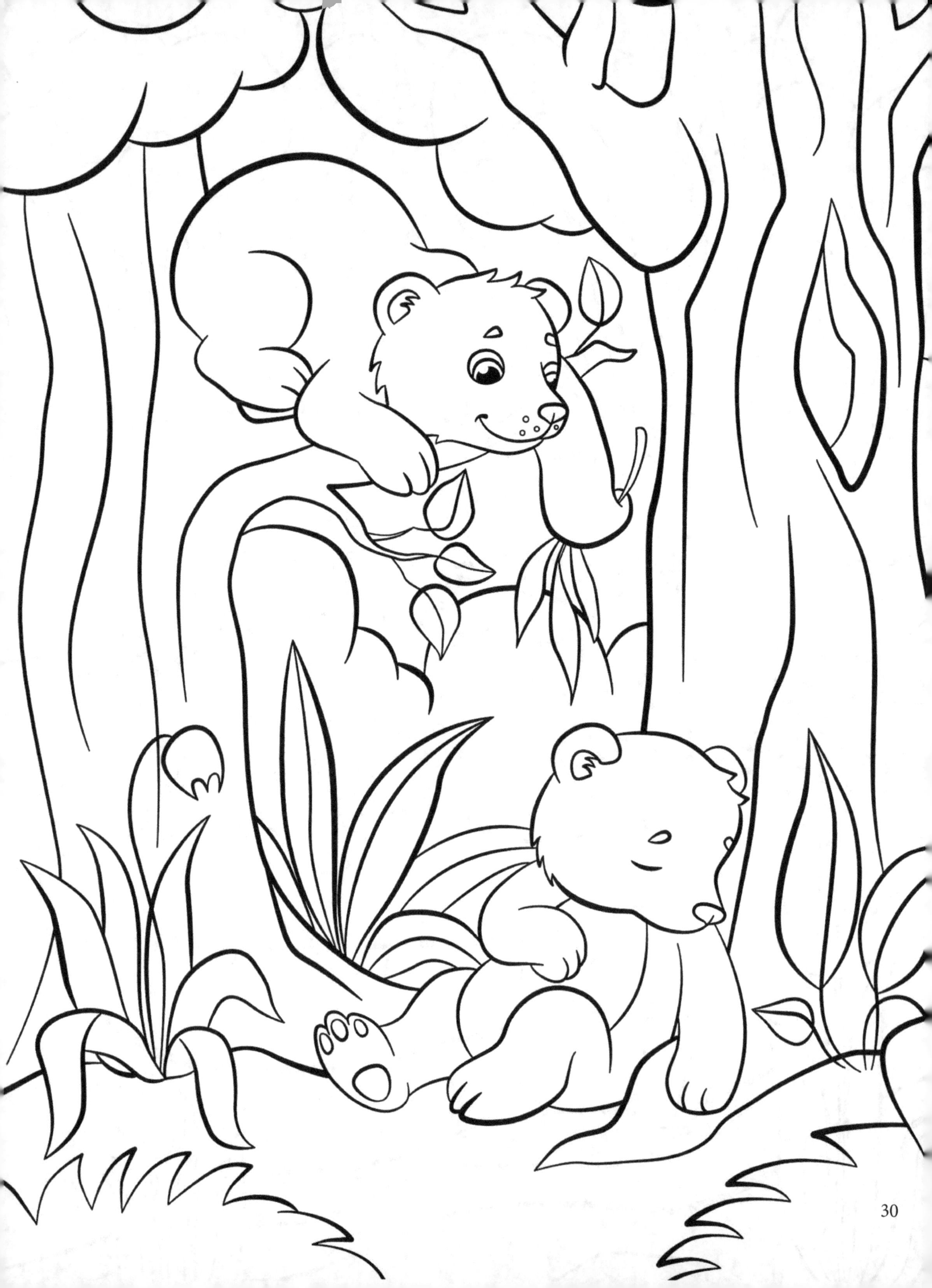

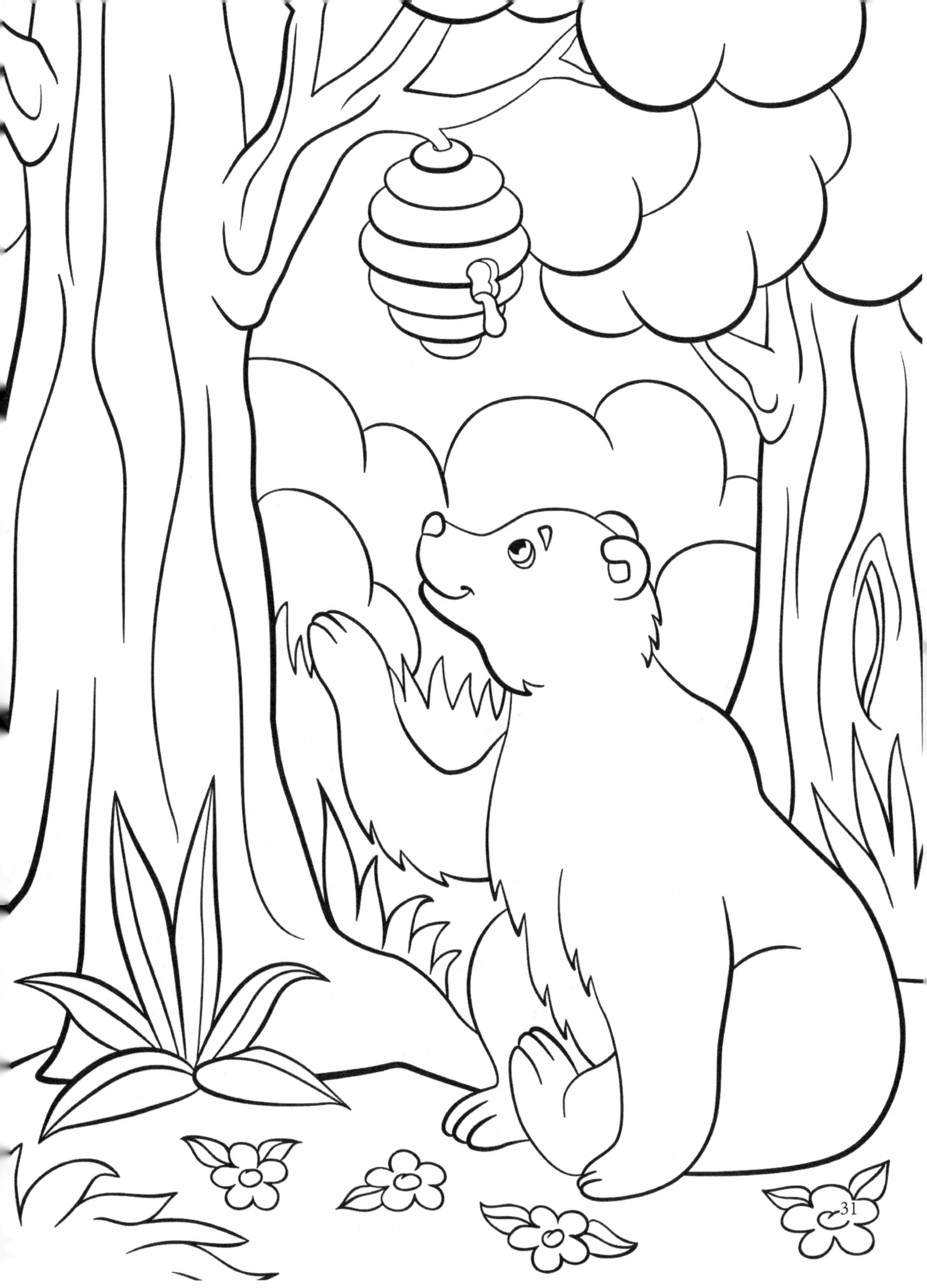

31

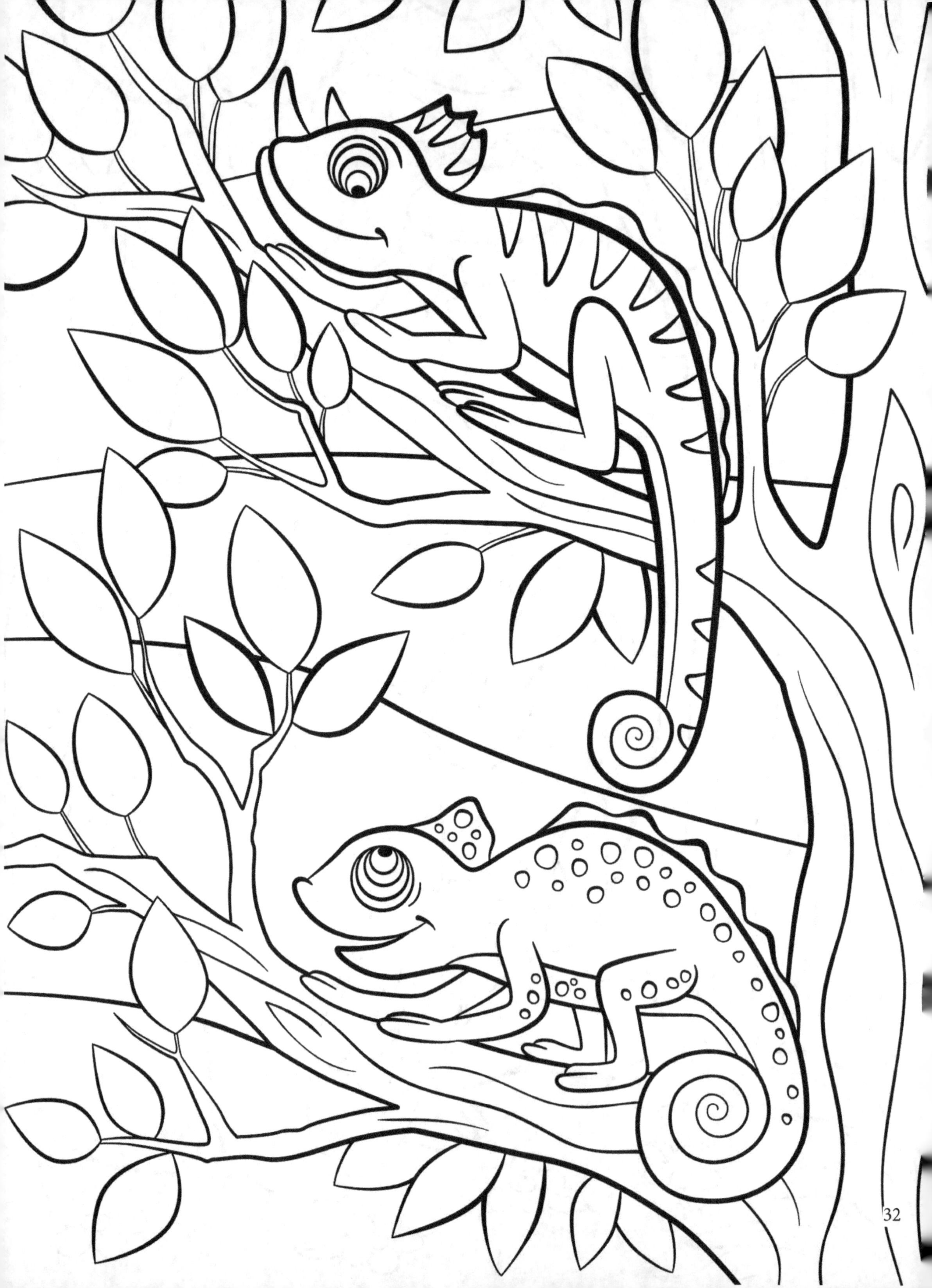

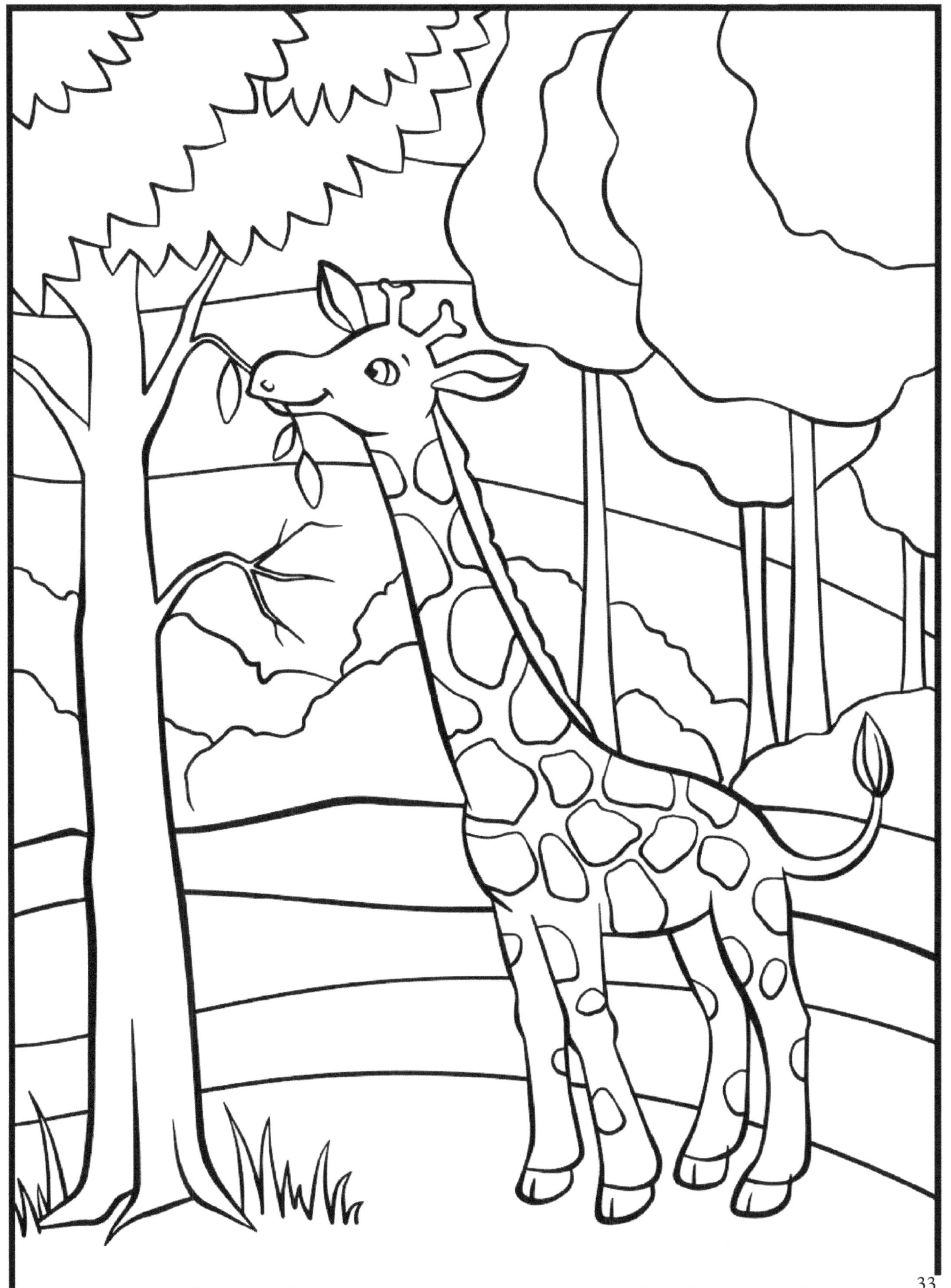

www.ingramcontent.com/pod-product-compliance
Lightning Source LLC
Chambersburg PA
CBHW081652060726
47593CB00023B/2773